THE

HAPPY & MARRIED

BOOK

**THE SECRET TO A RELATIONSHIP THAT
DARES TO SPEAK A DIFFERENT LANGUAGE**

JASON AND KELLI ANDERSON

Jason and Kelli Anderson are Lead Pastors at The Living Word Bible Church

www.livingwordonline.org

Copyright © 2018

THE HAPPY & MARRIED BOOK

- *I don't know what she wants. I don't know where he's going.* Dare to speak the language of your desires.

- *I'm upset about 4,000 different things; I don't even know where to start!* Renewal through the language of remembering.

- *All she does is argue and complain. He is ignoring me again!* Dare to speak the language of kindness.

- *We have the same problems we had last year!* The power of true transformation through God's language.

- *I'm exhausted from the criticism.* Learn the language that will elevate your spouse higher.

- *The only time we touch is for sex.* Dare to speak the forgotten language of affection.

- *We used to have a spark! Where did it go? How do we get it back?* Dare to speak the language of passion.

- *I'm not as happy as I thought I would be.* Learn to speak the language of your marriage expectations.

- *Men are from Neptune! Women are from Saturn!* Understanding each other is simple and possible.

- *My love cup is empty; I'm bankrupt on the inside.* Love is a river, not a cup.

PREFACE

There are a lot of great books on marriage filled to the brim with good information. They are often disguised in psychological and heady sounding phrases. This is not that book. Problem is, we didn't fall in love in our heads, it happened in the heart. Marriage grows like an organic plant. It is breathing. It is cultivated and nurtured in the rich soil of our hearts. Our words are the seeds. We set out to write a book about marriage that sought to identify how to plant the right garden for your marriage future. How can someone be happy and married? We want both. If words can build and grow, and our long conversations have much to do with our early love, maybe we already know the right language. I call it a *secret language* since the world has abandoned it.

God has anointed your marriage for peace. There is a supernatural marriage that you can receive from the Lord. He is a miracle working God. You are going to win. You are, in this moment, investing in your future. Things are about to get better for you. Whether things are going great or maybe your marriage needs surgery, just reading this line has you moving in the right direction. Why? God wants your life to get better, and He's positioning you right now because you have decided to get some new information, and He loves that. One of the ways Jesus brought change was by bringing the world some new information. He was always teaching. His words weren't for your head either. He said, "My words are spirit and they are life." Not head. Heart. This is where we are going. This is what makes this book different, and it also makes the adventure you are about to take different.

My wife and I are writing this together, so when we say "I" or "me" we mostly mean "we", and it could be either one of us in that moment speaking to you. We are drawing on decades of praying with and coaching a pool of diverse backgrounds and situations in marriage. We are also pulling from our experiences of being married for many, many, many years... year after year... and another year. *Wait, where was I?* We are super happily married. Not every year has been perfect and we've had our share of battles that you can relate to. Mostly, we build each sentence of this book on the wisdom we have learned from God's inescapable unadulterated truth, that is, the Word of God. I may not quote every Scripture, but if you're listening for it, you will hear the Word of God resonating.

In this book we are going to present topics and principles that will have your marriage speaking a new language, one that actually works. In the coming chapters we will look at some of the most discussed issues in marriage.

CONTENTS

DEDICATION AND ACKNOWLEDGEMENT

To our children. Parents were never so proud as we are. Greater things, far greater things will you do...

Chapter One

Dare to Speak a Different Language

"When I chose my wife, I didn't think of who I could live with — but who I didn't want to live without. And this was an easy decision for me. I did not want to live my life without her."
Creflo Dollar - Married since 1986

Spoken words move us in a direction. It's how we were created. God started the universe with words. Do you remember the first time you said *I love you*? Or maybe the first time you said *divorce*? Earth shattering. It shook your soul. Words can transport us to a new place. Words have power. They can alter our future, change our perspective, and move mountains. The world has taught us how to speak, but frankly, it is the wrong language. The contravening speech we are surrounded with divides us. What if we dared to speak a different language? Would it *really* matter? Can changing the words we say transport us somewhere new? Can words create a life we hate or a life we love?

There is a secret language that can catapult our marriage into a place higher than we thought possible; a marriage that is more than we can ask, think, dream, or imagine. In this book we dare to speak a different language. We are going to be learning many easy to remember principles to God's best for your life. We will be revisiting often the idea that the language we are speaking is directing our outcome. How do we talk about each other? How do we talk to each other? Do we talk?

We are going to begin this book by addressing how we communicate since what comes out of our mouths has so much power. Words can build up or tear down. What we say has the power of life and death. In the next chapter we will look at renewing our marriage. You may feel like renewal happens first, but be patient. This first practical approach to get us talking is going to stir in a great deal of hope for your future. After this we will continue through the book as we unlock principle after principle that will lead you down some very simple roads towards the milk and honey God has for your marriage. First things first though, let us look at our communication by introducing a simple problem.

Problem:
>   He wants to know what you are thinking...
>   She wants to know where you are going...

My wife and I both find this problem exists nearly across the board in relationships. It is a much boiled down statement, but significant and important to address. He doesn't really know what you want, and she doesn't really know where you are going. This can be solved. Studies have shown that the vast majority of fights in a marriage are directly related to simple poor communication. We just aren't talking.

Have you ever found yourself saying some of these things?

He doesn't know the kids routines/lives.
He forgets everything.

His family is annoying.
We need a plan, there is no plan!!!

What did she buy?
Sometimes I just want a thank you; she is so ungrateful!

He makes me feel worthless, unattractive.
She makes me feel dumb, unwanted.

He helps wrong – That's not how you wash dishes! Did I marry a 2 year old?
He doesn't just listen; instead he's always trying to fix me.

He's unhappy and I don't know why.
She's changing, and I don't know what is happening.

I don't know what she wants.
I don't know where he's going.

So let's talk about talking. Remember when you were first discovering each other? *Dating.* It was those deep conversations lying in the grass staring at the stars. "What do you want from this life?" We were digging in to the desires of each other's hearts. But now life is crazy. The only reason we lie down in the grass is because we tripped over the toy little Jimmy forgot to put away. "JIMMMY!" At some point we stopped sharing the big things. There isn't time, and if I have time to lie down, it's because I'm sleeping.

And so we are not talking. Usually one of the spouses is okay with not talking. This is because if we aren't talking it all is getting pent up inside. Then suddenly, when we finally are talking, we fight. So for some it's just easier to not talk; less pressure. But if we don't talk enough it can get serious. And so it finally happens, the dreaded, "We need to talk." Uh oh. The "We need to talk" talk happens because we haven't been talking all along.

Then we talk it all out sometimes, and then everything is better for a little while. "Are you guys doing better?"
"Yeah... we talked."

What we need is to put our talking into a routine.

If you want to get in shape you need a routine. You need a set time you work out every week. You will need a work out plan that is repeating. "Bi's and tri's on Monday and Thursday, chest and legs on Wednesday and Friday." A planned work out that repeats creates momentum towards your goal. If you don't set up a routine and only try and work out "when you can," well, you and I both know, it will never happen. The work out, though you want to do it and you want the result, will get drowned out by the random life.

There is a couple who were buying many things on credit because they could afford the payments. They both worked days. The money was just barely enough each month, but he could relieve that pressure by picking up an extra shift on Sundays and switching his shift to nights. After about six months of this they realized the marriage had lost some flavor, some buzz. There was a lot of snipping at each other. He was tired a lot. She was feeling neglected. He was doing it for her, to give her the best life he could. He was tired and felt unappreciated. What was more important to her than having nice things was having time with her husband. He had led them somewhere she did not want to go. Now they were in crisis mode. She had grown close to a guy she worked with. She could vent on him. So I asked her, "What do you want?" She wanted her husband to not have to work nights.

He replied, "Well, I don't want to work nights, but I did it for you." Problem solved. Neither wants him to work nights. They began working out toward what they both wanted. You see the problem was as simple as just not identifying what each other wanted. Talking.

I knew another couple who called and asked me what I thought about his wife transferring in her profession as a lawyer to traveling the world setting up new law offices on behalf of the partnership. She was going to do it. He was against it. What did I think? *It really doesn't matter what I think*, I told them. What does your wife want? The new position wasn't offering more money, so what was calling to her? I asked him to really drive in to his wife's heart about this. "You have to find out what the goal is in her heart. What does she want? She may not really fully know what she wants. The deep desires of our own hearts sometimes require digging," I explained. God *and* she want her to have the desires of her heart, and you do too. What is that desire? She has developed a solution to something, but to what? To fulfill what desire?

She wanted to see the world. She wanted vacations. Uh-oh. They were not taking vacations. He was always saying, "There is no time for a vacation." They would get a three day weekend at the most, and always somewhere convenient. Once this came out, they were able to decide that the new position wasn't the right solution, but that he needed to take her to Fiji (or something). He began to look at exotic far away lands with her and get himself mentally adjusted to fulfill the dreams of his wife's heart. Now don't get me wrong, they didn't just turn their life into a vacation every month, but a nice new location a couple times a year became a catalyst in their marriage for newness, romance, and growth. In fact, just setting the goal and having hope for the future immediately transformed their marriage.

Principle 1: Dare to speak the language of your desires.

I recommend a weekly meeting. *I know, I know*, it sounds so *not* spontaneous or romantic. It sounds so corporate. So don't take my meaning that way. This is about discovering desires *and* developing momentum towards the desires in your heart. What we want from this life will change constantly, but communicate your desires. Ladies, your husband really does want to know what you want. It will help him figure out where to go. There is great passion in discovery. You will find great romance in reinvention. Since we are each always changing, and each new season unlocks new things God has placed in us, we are going to be digging around for the desires in each other, finding where those desires merge, and helping each other get there. Now that sounds like a great meeting, doesn't it? Here we look at the simple questions:

1. So what does she want?
2. Where is he going?

Ladies, so often we just don't know what you really want. We will do it, but we need to know what *it* is. Husbands, can you just tell us where you are going? Is there some sort of plan?

Imagine that a couple is in a car headed somewhere. He asks

his wife as he pulls out into traffic, "Where do you want to eat?" It is an example of identifying what she wants. He has to ask.

She looks at her phone to see an incoming message and replies sounding a bit distracted, "Oh, I don't care." Hmm, he still doesn't know what she wants.

"Okay, burger or Mexican food?" He presses her.

"I want something new." He's is slowing down for the next light, a loud motorcycle is right on his tail. "Figures." He says annoyingly.

"What?" She demands as she looks up from her phone. From her expression he can tell something just went wrong.

"Oh no," eyebrows are climbing into his hair and with a flustered tone he states, "I meant the guy behind me. He's all up in my business."

"Where are you going? Where are we?" She asks.

And so the drive is happening. Two people going somewhere. He wants to know what she wants. She wants to know where he has taken them. I find this very simple misunderstanding at the heart of many marriage issues. There is an easy fix. *Dare to speak the language of your desires.*

Schedule a time once per week where there is a leadership meeting in your marriage. Have a devoted communicating time. Just like you wouldn't miss a work meeting, or be late, you need a family leadership meeting. You need a romantic date every week as well, but this is not that meeting. Imagine a business where the leadership never meets because they are all too busy. So then one leader is busy working up data on a spreadsheet and the phone is ringing. Who is calling now? The other leader, his partner, is calling. No time to talk now. He answers, but she begins asking about something completely unrelated and wants a meeting. But now is not a good time. This company will not do well. This company will be bankrupt soon. Marriages that don't meet often find themselves feeling bankrupt.

Imagine a business where the leaders are communicating. The partners meet once per week to look at the vision, the goal, and the results. What do we want? Are we making progress? What can be done with our five-year-old and his misbehaving? Our teenage son, Ted, may need a science tutor. I don't like the look in the guest bath, can we paint it? When? I am out of town for work the second week in May. Isn't that when your sister Tanya is due to have her baby?

A great time to meet is early in the morning, before kids get up. Make her some eggs and coffee. Be up an hour early and communicate. Talk about dreams. Talk about desires and wants. Pray for the impossible. Keep a list of what you are up to. Have a calendar ready and communicate what is happening in each of your worlds. A husband and a wife have plenty to talk about. In the next chapter we want to talk about this meeting, some tips and tricks to making it successful and some insight to why communication can seem so impossible even when it isn't.

> Proverbs 11:14 (NIV) [14]For lack of guidance a nation falls, but victory is won through many advisers.

Here the advisors met. It is the same for your family. Victory comes through taking the time to sort through things and advise each other.

Consider that the trash man shows up on Tuesdays. Every Tuesday. Imagine if the trash truck couldn't come every

Tuesday, but they were getting to your house when there was time. Sometimes it's Wednesdays. Sometimes the truck didn't come that week. In the confusion you left your can out a day late. In my house, just one week of missed trash pickup and we are overflowing. We get stopped up. The backyard where the cans sit begins to smell. This is happening in marriages when there are no routines. We get stopped up. It really has nothing to do with how hard each is trying, or how much each loves each other; it is just a matter of busy life.

You need a weekly meeting. Yes, I mean weekly. Your weekly communication meeting needs to be on the schedule as a set routine. I know a couple who goes to breakfast and then a short hike or walk every Friday morning. They have a system that works for the kids that day, and work has it handled so they come in just a bit later. Since they started doing this, they have noted a massive change in misunderstandings, fights, confusion, and also their attitudes and energy. After just a few months things in the relationship started to change. The direction of marriage, health, finances, and children, all of it began to gain momentum. It's not a date. It is a meeting. On your date you can refrain from errands and discussing the busy-ness of life, and instead you can be romantic. If there is no meeting we often vomit a bunch of communication on the date, which is a quick way to ruin that date, and get some future dates cancelled. No, the date is different than the meeting. The meeting figures out desires and direction. What does she want? Where is he going?

So, you've scheduled your weekly meeting. Your marriage is your marriage, so how you do this will be on you, what works for you, but I do offer some simple guidelines and wisdom. First, let us talk about listening!

Principle 2: The Secret Language of Listening

The most giving and selfless part of communication is listening. This is a secret lost language, the form of communication where one doesn't speak, but engages to pursue what the other is truly trying to convey.

> Romans 10:17 (NIV) [17]Consequently, faith comes from hearing the message, and the message is heard through the word about Christ.

Our covenant with God is not held together by love, but by faith. He loves us. He poured His love into us. Without His love we cannot love in His way. His love casts out fear and never fails. But it is our faith that accesses the covenant with God. Our faith in Jesus is why we are in covenant with the Living God. Faith. Likewise, marriage is a covenant. Our covenant in marriage is also not held together by love. Lots of people loved each other but were divorced. The separation happens as we stop believing in each other. You stop believing that your spouse is right for you, or can ever make you truly happy. You stop believing they love you, or have been faithful. These are deal breakers for most. The covenant of marriage, it is held together by faith. It is glued together by believing in one another. When you believe in your spouse you release the power that is in them to invade your life. It is the same as you believe in God. Your faith in God releases His power into your world. Faith.

Faith comes by hearing. Talking is important too, but I want you to understand the magnitude of hearing. Hearing will birth faith in you. You know your husband loves you, but then he looks into your soul, he stops joking around for one second, and he grabs your hand with his hands firmly but lovingly, and spins you into facing him. Suddenly you are flashing back to a moment with him when you were dating, your heart is pounding, and he says, "Baby, I really do love you." Fireworks. Did you hear him? Faith was just now built. She may know it, but man, she needs to hear it.

Listening then is key.

> 1 John 4:7 (TPT) [7]"Those who are loved by God, let his love continually pour from you to one another, because God is love. Everyone who loves is fathered by God and experiences an intimate knowledge of him."

Everyone wants to be respected and valued for who they are. You are a unique person, with unique gifts and unique talents. People gain value and feel loved when we take time to hear them. This is especially true in marriage. When we seek to listen to others we seek to understand and not to judge. I correlate listening to compassion. When Jesus was moved with compassion, he was moved to listen to the needs of the people. It was Jesus who took a whole different route to Jerusalem, went through Samaria, just to talk to a woman at the well. She was hurting, broken, and probably completely hated who she was. But, Jesus came and listened to her. He was more interested in the matters of her heart than anything else. He knew what would change her life; the living waters that never run dry. Jesus loved her in this moment. We can draw on that same love that God has poured into our lives. God is love and His love is poured into our lives daily. When we take the time and listen, we step into love.

What is it that makes someone a good listener? First, they're present. A Greek philosopher, Epictetus said, "We have two ears and one mouth so we can listen twice as much as we speak." A great listener is mindful of where they are and who they are talking to. When you are fully aware of the moment, you are more likely to retain what you're hearing and in turn you will naturally respond with more authenticity. This means stashing the phones and ridding yourself of all distractions. I call it going airplane mode. (My brother and I actually call it this.) When you fly on an airplane they make you put your phone into airplane mode during the take-off and landing. This cuts down on some kind of interference, or is maybe just the airlines way of annoying all of us. Airplane mode means your phone will not receive any data, messages, or phone calls. It is literally useless in airplane mode. It cannot distract you. You cannot surf social networking or text or make a call. When you refuse any outside distraction because of what you are up to, this is airplane mode. Make your conversation with your spouse "airplane mode." Put that thing down. Our phones can be so loud in our lives. They vibrate or make a sound and no matter what we are doing we are suddenly compelled to look at them. If someone is talking to you, you could be totally still listening, but as you look at your device you appear as though something is more important than they are. This isn't true. Of course it isn't true, but it is what it looks like. You may be one of those people that can totally hold a conversation while texting, and I applaud that. Still, imagine the value someone feels when you take the conversation airplane mode. You are saying, "I am interested in what you are saying, I am listening, and I'm not about to let anything distract me from that."

Great listeners are empathetic. Part of effective listening is the effort to empathize with the person you're speaking with. Whether you can relate or not, the compassion won't go unnoticed. As you are listening, spend a moment putting yourself in their position. What's going on in their head? What must it be like to be them? And, as you are listening, ask the Holy Spirit to reveal to you understanding.

> Proverbs 5:1 (NIV) [1]"Let the wise listen and add to their learning, and let the discerning get guidance."

We need the Holy Spirit to reveal to us understanding and to show us the other person's deepest needs. We are able to listen to his or her true feelings, to discern them, and to understand. Let the wise listen and add to their understanding. The understanding comes by the listening. Jesus was the truest picture of a great listener. He had compassion for everyone. Listening helps meet the deepest need of a man and a woman which is to feel loved, wanted, and accepted.

A great listener realizes their own shortcomings. This may be a strange way of thinking, but accepting YOURSELF is a key to being a good listener. I may not always have the answer when I'm listening to my spouse. And, I'm ok with that. But, I may be the bridge to the answer. Sometimes the best answer is prayer. You don't have to solve your spouse's problems or situations. You just need to point them in the right direction. And that's ALWAYS Jesus.

> Hebrews 12:1-2 (NIV) [1]Let us throw off everything that hinders and the sin that so easily entangles. [2]And let us run with perseverance the race marked out for us, fixing our eyes on Jesus, the pioneer and perfecter of faith...

When we focus on Jesus, He will always take us to the place

of victory in our lives. He will always lead you in the right direction. You don't have to have some great answer. The greatest answer is turning to prayer and to Jesus. Every conversation you have isn't going to solve the larger issue. But it puts you closer to understanding each other. Again, when we are listening, we are seeking to understand. Draw on the Holy Spirit to gain perspective, wisdom, and understanding. And, you know, sometimes you just need to listen to your spouse and that's it. Just listen. I have found this with our children. Sometimes they just need you to listen to them. I have found this with our daughter.

She exclaims to me, "Mom! I don't need you to solve the problem; I just want to tell you what's going on!"

She just needed me to listen. Once she gives me the problem, I can now pray that she finds the answer. I don't need to be her Jesus. Again, the solution will always be pointing them to Jesus, the Word.

Effective communicating and listening isn't just lending your ear, but asking appropriate follow-up questions to draw out more information. *So, what you're saying is...So let me make sure I'm hearing you correctly...Is this what you're saying?*

Funny thing is, sometimes what we hear is not what they're saying.

Husband: "So, what you're saying is this..."
Wife: "That's not even close to what I said. This is what I said..."

Remember we are seeking to understand the other person. This does take time and practice. I still to this day, after twenty five years of learning my husband, will ask follow up questions! Half the time I will hear my spouse correctly, the other half of the time they will have to correct my interpretation.

Another aspect to effective listening is practicing the art of self-control over your own mouth. It's easy to want to jump into a conversation and completely derail the entire thing! Have you ever been talking to someone, they asked you the question, you are responding, and in the middle of your response they jump in, "Oh, this one time I was just standing at the…"? You literally did not finish your thought or explanation, and now you are watching a completely different film featuring them! A great listener will allow the other to fully speak what they desire, keeping in my mind how they will want to respond, but not interrupting to get their voice heard.

Do you know what happens when you allow a person to fully express their conversation to you? Their heart is revealed to you. Look at Matthew 12:34 (NKJV) where Jesus said, "…for out of the abundance of the heart, the mouth speaks." When our son Mathew was about 14 years old, we noticed that he just didn't seem himself. He seemed to be carrying the weight of the world on his shoulders. He was grumpy and snippy with all of us. This went on for several days. "What's your problem??"

"Nothing!" He snapped back. This was very unusual behavior for him. He's the super goofy and really outgoing kid in our home.

So, Kelli and I said to him, "We need to talk!" We went up to his room and we started asking him questions. What's going on Mat? Are you ok? Is something going on in school? Are you dealing with a drama with a friend? What is it? All he kept saying to us was, "No," to every single question. I think he knew we weren't leaving his room until we got an answer. Then the Holy Spirit kicked in. "You know, Mat, we just want the very best for you in your life. We think that you are the greatest, smartest, most talented, super good looking, kid around." All of a sudden, it was like the wall around his heart came down, and the flood began to happen. Out of the abundance of the heart, the mouth spoke. And we just sat there. We didn't comment and we didn't interrupt. We allowed the issues of the heart to be exposed. Now we knew the things he had been dealing with. And, now we could point him to Jesus. Once he had exposed it all, we now were able to correct.

This leads me to the next point. A good listener is not on the defensive. Not all things you are going to hear are going to be a thornless rose garden filled with ice cream vendors. Effective listeners don't block out negative criticism. Instead they listen and develop an understanding of what the person is trying to convey, before responding.

> James 1:19 (NIV) [1]...Everyone should be quick to listen, slow to speak and slow to become angry.

In addition to not playing defense, embrace every emotion during your conversations. Embrace even the feelings of discomfort or anger. Some of the greatest breakthroughs in my life in the area of relationships are when I got really uncomfortable; when I allowed my guard to come down and I listened to the people in my life. It got super uncomfortable because I allowed the other person to honestly reveal their heart to me. And in that moment, I can correct what may have been a misunderstanding or ask forgiveness of something I've done or said to bring hurt into their life.

Next, not only do we need to become expert listeners, but we also need to know and understand the desires of our lover. This can be tricky. God wants to give us the desires of our heart, that is, He placed those desires in there, and it is how He gets us to partner with what He wants to do. In this it becomes important to go digging for desire. What I mean is, often we don't actually know what we want, and in what order those desires land. Asking questions to help each other find what they truly desire becomes important and rewarding. If you want to dig around and really know someone, begin to ask them about what they want in this life. What is important to you? When a husband asks his wife, "Baby, what do you truly want?"

"I just want to feel loved," She says. Or "I feel like the kids are growing up to fast!" Or "I am tired of never having enough." Now the two can develop a plan to help move in that direction. If she's tired of not having enough, maybe you guys can start figuring out a way to start that business, even if you have to start super small. Does she not feel loved? Ask her what you can do to make her feel what you know to be true. "I want our family in church." Well jeez, that's not a big one. You just didn't know it was so important, that it was a desire of her heart. Husbands are great at goals and solutions. Wives are great at identifying opportunities for strengthening. Communication will make a big difference here. This means a main priority for each is to identify and actively involve yourself in helping the other attain the desire of their heart. There is a deep desire in you already, a God-given desire, to give your spouse their desires.

In 2018 we celebrated our son Logan's 11th birthday at Disneyland. We were in California on vacation, and Disney is always a must for our family. The family enjoyed an incredible day of short lines and churros. Toward the end of the day Logan said he wanted to see the early showing of the much sought after "Fantasmic." Almost everyone wants to see this show, and viewing space is limited. The show is outside, so you just find a spot in the park where you can see, and then you stand and wait for it to begin. If you want a decent spot, you show up about two hours early. Attending this show means crowds, massive, massive, crowds. (And yes, we know all about fast passes, we are pros.) If you haven't heard, over the years we have learned about the dining experiences that can reserve you a really good spot to see some of the bigger shows. These dining experiences need reservations months in advance. We didn't have a reservation... so we prayed. We walked up to one of the restaurants at around five in the afternoon to see if they had a table open for the show at eight that night. The employee at first flashed an eye roll at our request, "Sir, these tables are reserved in advance and... (pause as she looks at her notebook), wait, is this right?" She asks the employee next to her. There was a cancellation. A table for five had just opened up for the show. Perfect.

We ate wonderfully, then sat and enjoyed a crowd free experience of "Fantasmic." Just as the show ended the fireworks started, and the table we were at seemed to be a perfect. We saw it all! After the fireworks, Logan looks at me with a dreamy look in his eyes and a smile frozen to his face. He had my full attention. He spoke in staccato, spacing his words out perfectly, "BEST – BIRTHDAY – EVER!" Those three words made an eternal impression in my heart. A trophy. We won. I want this same reaction from my wife as we stand in eternity before Jesus. I want her to look at Jesus and say "BEST – HUSBAND – EVER." Make that a desire. Make that a goal.

So on to the mechanics of our meeting: Start your meeting with prayer. I recommend you make a basic list of things you are praying over every week. You might pray for things like your children, that they have the right friends, and that their future spouse is set apart for them. Pray for health and safety. Pray over your finances. There are many books on effective prayer. Pick some up and read about how Jesus taught us to pray. After adding something new to the prayer list one of us will find a Scripture that has something to do with our prayer. For instance, when we pray for our kids we declare, "Lord, you said you would bless us and our children. We are standing in faith for our children because we know you are faithful to your promise."

It is beneficial to pray the Scripture, to have faith, and to declare God's promises into your family. I know a couple who made a list to pray at my advice. The list said things like "Help my husband not be so selfish." *So, yeah, not that kind of list.* Prayer gets us into hope!

Next, do some goal setting. Goal setting is important for success and movement in every situation. Whether you're playing sports or starting a business, goals get us up in the morning. Goals should be on your weekly meeting list, and not crossed off until they are attained. Goals are broken into tasks that each can work on. "Hey can you make the call this week to get that reservation? I'll go online and search for the football pads to see if we can save some money there. What if we train Johnny to do his own laundry? I mean, he's fifteen-years-old now. He can do it. Heck, he does trigonometry. That way when he runs out of shirts, well, it's on him. Oh, can you call the dentist today?"

Have some goals you discuss. Focus on the movement towards those goals. Stay hopeful. Ask each other questions like, "What can we do this week to move us toward these things?" Maybe you want to work on little Johnny's math grades. How are you going to do that? What night do you have time? Get out a calendar and look at dates of things coming up. Many times we double book things and create all kinds of fights just from not telling each other what is going on.

Husbands, be aware that a wife is greatly moved by things that are moving in a hopeful direction. My wife lived in a house with no furniture for almost two years. During this time I was paying down all of our years of dating debt. As long as my wife saw progress on that debt, and had furniture magazines to look at, or was perusing through furniture stores to get ideas, she was great. People can wait as long as they see movement.

Discuss solutions. Notice I didn't say to discuss problems. Really, I'm saying to try your best to bring up problems as opportunities. Now this may sound really impossible, but it isn't. You still need this time to discuss how her mom is really upsetting you, or how you are sick of driving that cruddy broken car. There are problems, and we need to meet about them, but how you say it matters. Listen, you're finally communicating, don't mess that up! We all naturally avoid discomfort. For this reason we are looking for a positive and hopeful time at the meeting. You won't keep meeting if the meeting is just a mudslinging festival. Keep the gloves up at all costs. There is a time for complaining and expressing anger, but not at the meeting. By all means, have a good fight some other time, when it's fresh and raw, but not at the meeting. You want to be solutions minded, pray about problems, worries, anxious things. Pray about the future. Give to God those things that appear impossible. Encourage one another. Find a way to solve the recurring problems permanently.

Your goal for your meeting is about your spouse! What I mean is their goals become your goals. We need to keep the walls down and the gates wide open. Remember we enter gates with thanksgiving in our hearts. We enter the courts with praise. If you want to dig for the wants and desires in your spouse, you do it through thanksgiving and praise. If you have thirty things to complain about and can think of only one thing you are thankful for, well, go with the one. A simple way to keep your spouse open is when:

He feels wanted, successful, believed in, trusted, and confident in where he is going.
She feels valued, safe, attractive, hopeful, and understood in what she wants.

Last, having a meeting agenda is very important. This will record your goals, your prayer list, and anything that you thought of during the time between meetings. As your week goes on things will come up that need to be in the meeting. If possible, just jot them down on your agenda to be addressed later. Timing happens to be one of the most complained about communication issues in marriage. A husband is watching sports (classic example) and she suddenly wants to have a 30 minute conversation about how she is thinking of quitting her job next week. She feels like he values a bunch of men dressed like twinkies playing catch more than the mother of his children. He is annoyed because he had an hour *before the game started* to talk while she was staring at her phone. If it's a common fight, then beat it once and for all. Never have this fight again. Husband, turn off the tv immediately to let her know she is the most important thing in your life. Wives, put it down on the agenda and let it go. Let him turn his show back on. Maybe make him some popcorn.

A much better example than this though... A husband is at work and she calls. "What is your plan with little Jimmy?! Do you know what he did this morning???!"

He's derailed. He's thinking, "Seriously? Now? You want to do this now?" Men are very laser focused. One thing at a time. At the job we really are designed to be in warrior mode, hunting and taking over the world. My mind leaves the house about an hour before I do, as I prepare for success that day. A man's mind develops momentum as it ponders a certain thing. This is why sometimes it might seem to our wives we can't hear. We seem incapable of multi-tasking. You see, when you burst into that question, your husband was half way through his work presentation that he is giving next week. He was doing it all in his mind. *Let's see, if I give the analysis first, and then go to my statement, it might sound like...* Suddenly his eyes rifle to lock with yours saying, "Wait, sorry, what, what did you just say?" Later when you're at work you suddenly remembered something you need to discuss with him and so you reach out to him on the phone. It isn't that he doesn't want to field your phone call or text at 10am, and it also has nothing to do with how much he loves you or thinks about you. He is just built to thwart distractions. If at all possible put new problems or discussions on the agenda for your next scheduled meeting. You will avoid many fights by putting things that can wait onto your agenda. In this way you are guaranteed to have uninterrupted scheduled time to really discuss the problem. After adding it to the agenda, let it go. I still think you should call and say, "Hey I'm just leaving for work now, Jimmy has some issues I want to talk about at our meeting on Friday, but don't worry about it for now, go kick it today honey, knock it out. You're the best!"

A meeting agenda can help you have a much more positive week in your marriage. There will be some things that can't wait, of-course. But if you can limit the number of fires that are blowing up throughout the week, and move much of the discussion to your weekly meeting, your conversations will make a natural move away from the business of the family, and have time to explore the treasure of the family. You will leave behind the language of the family business dominating every conversation, and give space to the language of love. When this happens, something quite magical invades your family atmosphere, and you will find it magnetic.

In this chapter we created a plan for intentionally talking and meeting that if followed can eliminate more than 50% of marriage conflict. That's big. We are learning to speak a new kind of language, one that most will neglect or see as frivolous, but not you. God is showing you even now the power of hope and desire working in your relationship. The happiest marriage in the world can be yours, and it is a gift from God. In love. One. In the next chapter we delve into renewing, resetting, and repositioning your relationship for victory. Are you ready? Great, here we go.

Chapter Two

Renewal Through the Language of Remembering

"My secret to a great marriage is that every single day I look at my wife and find a reason to fall in love with her that day."
Pastor Kevin Messner – Married since May 4, 1991

The goal of this chapter is simple. We want to restart and renew your marriage through the power of remembering. There are things that we will remember, and other things that we will no longer remember. We are going to learn a new language in our memory. We are going to imitate the Lord here.

Can I ask you a question? I want to go back in your memories to the beginning. Do you remember the first time you saw him? The first time you met her? What was the first thing that went through your mind? Take a moment and relive the story. Tell me, how did you meet? When did you know they were *the one?* What funny thing did he do on the first date? I

25

remember something funny I did on our first date. I was holding my glass of water at dinner and decided to check my watch to see how long we had until our movie started. I was so smooth. So cool. Suit jacket. Fancy restaurant. Valet parking. As I turned my hand over to see my watch I dumped the water right into my lap. Yeah, that just happened. Luckily she only laughed at me for, well, actually, she's still laughing about it.

It is interesting that when we "remember" the right things, it does amazing things to our emotions. This is to become the new language of our memory.

> Philippians 4:8 (NIV) [4]Finally, brothers and sisters, whatever is true, whatever is noble, whatever is right, whatever is pure, whatever is lovely, whatever is admirable--if anything is excellent or praiseworthy--think about such things.

In the same way, when we remember the wrong things, we can stir ourselves up into anger and frustration, hopelessness, and discouragement. This is the language we don't speak anymore. It is destructive. You can make yourself mad again about something that happened long ago. You know the same person you are married to now is the same person you chose to marry. Sometimes we find ourselves years into our marriage with all kinds of walls between us. There is resentment, or we've become just so easily annoyed; it didn't used to feel like this. What's the difference? What is the difference between the day we were married and the walls we have all this time later? The difference is all the negative stuff you remember about your spouse. There, I said it. The words from the fights are still lingering in your mind. The times he made you feel worthless. The moments she rejected you and made you feel unwanted. Negative moments become walls, barriers. Okay, so what then is the solution? If you are mad about 4,000 individual items it can seem like you're at a point of no return. Unfixable. *There are so many things, where do I begin?*

Principle 3: What you choose to remember matters.

To look at how your marriage can grow into all that God wants it to be, we must first be willing to look at and abandon the failed strategies we have been trying. Or...We can continue on a normal course and finally, through our complaining, get our spouse to change into what we need them to be.... Let's try that now.

I have an idea. (I'm kidding) Complain about all the negative things about your spouse and then hope they change. This is what society has taught us to do with things we don't like. This is the world's language for marriage. Truth is, complaining is powerless. Your complaining just won't change a thing about them. Complaining is exactly what you do when you think you cannot change something. We complain about our schools, our government, our job, the weather, and anything we aren't in a position of authority to change. If Goliath is making a stink on the battlefield, you could be like the rest of the army and complain, or you could be David, who didn't complain, but instead asked what would happen if he were to solve the problem and slay Goliath. (Goliath here is a problem in your marriage.) You are David. With God as your partner you can slay the Goliath. No more complaining. Has complaining worked? I asked a husband this question once.

I asked, "Now has complaining *to* her changed

anything *about* her?" The answer was, *no*. He would complain a lot. But that doesn't work. Now I'm not saying that you shouldn't communicate your expectations in marriage. I'm simply pointing out that it is hard to change someone, nay impossible, via the strategy of complaining. Now it may help for a few minutes. You can make life so painful for your spouse that they make minor adjustments just so they can breathe again. Still, it seems the change doesn't last, and you are back to the same old fight again.

We need to leave the old strategy of complaining. To abandon one strategy we need to replace it with a new strategy. Can we truly change each other? Is our crystal clear memory of the negative things and events about our spouse helping our marriage? Is my holding on to these things helping change my spouse? Can I change my spouse? Can I change myself? The answer is no. The Bible says in Philippians 1:6 (NIV) "being confident of this, that he who began a good work in you will carry it on to completion until the day of Christ Jesus." Who is He? Jesus. You chose Him right? Nope, He chose you. And He began a work in you. And HE will complete the work. Jesus can change us. In this chapter I will show you how God handles our shortcomings so that He has a perfect relationship with us. In this is the secret to complete renewal, transformation, and freedom in your relationship! So what is the real question? I think the real question is, how does God handle our failures and shortcomings? We could apply His tactics. His strategy will work. Let's learn to imitate our father; He certainly knows how to make this work.

Let us begin with memories. Do you need a reboot in your marriage? David writes in Psalms 18:16 (NKJV) "He sent from above, He took me; He drew me out of many waters." In other words, sometimes we are upset about so many things that it just is a big ball of tangled yarn. It's too many waters and your marriage is drowning.

"So *what's wrong*, you ask?" She says sarcastically, "Yeah, where do I even begin!!!"

But God can deliver your marriage from the many waters. How? Well, how did He deliver you? Your own personal life is full of many shortcomings, wrong decisions and wrong intentions. David said, "I was born sinful." Paul said, "Who will save me from this body of death?" So how does God do it? How does God overlook all of our sins? The answer is redemption. He forgives and forgets. Isaiah 43:25 (NKJV) "I, [even] I, [am] He who blots out your transgressions for My own sake; And I will not remember your sins."

Well look here, He does it for His own benefit. He does this so that He can have a close un-severable relationship with you, a relationship where your shortcomings are incapable of separating you from His love. And what does He say? He says, "I will not remember your sins." See, His decision. He just decided not to remember. You might be thinking, "That's impossible." Actually, it is impossible for God to forget, I mean probably. But it is His choice. It doesn't say He forgot. It says He does not remember. Why? Remembering our wrongs will build a barrier between us. Hmm. Now then, imitating this, God will give you the strength right now to do this very thing in your marriage.

God is delivering you from the many waters right now. It is by His strength. God is causing you to no longer remember all the negative things, the transgressions. Did you know a transgression is defined as one man sinning against another? You may have felt wronged in many ways. But now you are letting go, of all of it, because of God. Because of Christ you are remembering it no more. It's a brand new beginning. He says things like, "Don't let the sun go down on your anger," and "His mercies are new every day." This is you. Jesus in you has new mercies every day for your spouse. These mercies enable you to not see the bad, so that you can hone in on the good.

But what about justice? It's not fair what they did to you! Justice says, "Someone has to pay!" That's the reality. You have to punish them for what they have done to you! (Now if someone has done something illegal like beating a child, by all means, throw them in prison in order to protect others from the future abuses. But you can still let it all go emotionally!) The Lord says in Zechariah 7:9 (NKJV) "Thus says the LORD of hosts: 'Execute true justice, Show mercy and compassion Everyone to his brother." Real justice is when you decide on mercy. Jesus on the cross would totally have been justified in being angry at his killers, but instead, He applied mercy. He said, "Father forgive them..." Forgiving is for your freedom. But it is for God's sake. In others words, God forgives you for His own benefit. Are you getting this? It's absolutely brilliant. Genius. You forgive your spouse for your own benefit! It is for your happiness. It keeps you from withholding goodness. When we feel the need to punish we withhold goodness. But remember this one thing, Jesus paid for all sin. Even what they did to you was paid for by Christ. Now withhold no good thing.

Ponder this, as Paul wrote in Romans 2:4 (NKJV) "...the goodness of God leads one unto repentance." This is God's strategy. The normal way of handling a problem in a marriage is to begin withholding. We withhold our goodness. This pushes our marriage deeper into a spiral of unhappiness. One spouse puts in place the love embargo, forcing the other as well to begin withholding, and both are missing the fundamental and necessary pieces of marriage that define a marriage.

"Oh, you're going to do that are you? Well two can play at that game."

So we strive to get even, or to send a message to the other that we are fed up with their behavior. Now we really will get to the behavior later in this book, in fact in the very next chapter. For now what we are after, our entire goal of this chapter, is a complete reboot absent of baggage.

When the prophet Samuel announced Saul would be King, they couldn't find him. As they searched, the Bible says, "He has hidden himself among the baggage." God has called your marriage into His kingdom, into royalty. But like Saul, we can't step into all that God has called us up to as long as we keep hanging out with the baggage. If God can overlook our mess for the sake of the relationship, then so can we. He will give you the power.

There is a past, I know that, but what if right now you just reboot the whole thing?

You might be thinking, "Well I don't want to just be back in the same place in a month as we are now. Things have to change!"

I agree, and you won't be back in the same place in a month. You are going to have a new strategy, one that works. The Lord is breaking the cycle of the old patterns. He is releasing His power even now to overcome things you have not been able to do on your own strength. Jesus is expressing himself in you.

Realize this; you can't get to a renewed marriage without a good starting line. You just can't. Have you ever been working on your computer and it was slow, freezing over and over? It is so frustrating. It turns out that over time all sorts of programs and data get stuck in the computer memory. Eventually, and if you own a computer you know I'm right, you just have to reboot the whole thing. Suddenly it's humming along. Your phone can be the same. It has lost connection, can't text, websites won't load, and social media is down... so you restart your phone, and everything is suddenly as it should be.

God has a reset for you. Even if she has done the unthinkable, listen, you could have left, but you picked up this book because you want to make a go of it. If you are serious about making it work, this is a prerequisite. You have to live your marriage as though it never happened. You can literally never bring it up again. God is giving you the strength right now to let go of the past and have it drown in the sea of His forgetfulness. Say what God says:

> Isaiah 43:25 (NIV) [25]I, even I, am he who blots out
> your transgressions, for my own sake, and remembers
> your sins no more.

It is for your own sake. This is how we heal the relationship. God can't expect us to stop making mistakes in order to be close to us, so instead, He decides to not remember them. Many are reading this book to just tighten up their "already good" marriage. But there are some who are reading this book because they are holding on by a thread. If that is you, today you can both commit to a fresh start. It really is the only way. A fresh start means no baggage. Whatever is in the past, let it go, remember it no more, and let the Lord make all things new.

Redemption starts with blood. Jesus blood. Do you know what else starts with blood? Healing. If you cut yourself the first step to healing is bleeding. This is a picture of Jesus blood shed for us. To begin the healing process in marriage, we must start with the blood of redemption. Did you know that the reason each one of us acts well below our potential for goodness is because of our pain? The enemy tempts us in our pain. For instance, an alcoholic knows that the drinking is hurting themselves. So why does it continue? Pain. They drink because they are in pain. So a Christian says to an alcoholic, "Stop drinking, God doesn't want you to ruin your life." But still, they keep drinking. Why? Pain.

A promiscuous girl knows she shouldn't be allowing the wrong men in her life. But she is in pain. She is trying to fill the void an absent father left in her heart. It is an inescapable vacuum. But Jesus doesn't transform us by telling us what we are doing wrong. He transforms us by loving us and accepting us. Let me explain. God demonstrated His love in that while I wasn't even close to perfect, and I was deserving of punishment and wrath, he gave His only Son for me. The Bible goes on to say that if He wouldn't withhold His only son from me, then He will also give to me freely all things. II Peter 1:4 tells me that the promises of God will enable me to escape the corruption of this world caused by evil desires. Let me say it a different way; God's goodness is the catalyst of my transformation. How does this work? Well, one of His promises is that Jesus came to heal the broken hearts. He heals my pain. The cross provides healing for my heart. God's love heals the heart of this promiscuous girl I mentioned. When her heart is healed it changes her behavior. God is her Father now; an unconditional loving father. The vacuum is gone and she is free of the drive to fill that hole in her heart. When Jesus removes the pain from the alcoholic, he has no more reason to drink. You see, goodness leads us to repentance. Repentance is our changed behavior. We are transformed because He accepts us as we are. He loves us unconditionally. He withholds no good thing.

This means not only have you forgiven your spouse, but you are choosing to withhold nothing. You will no longer withhold your goodness. Goodness is released into your marriage. It is *so* contagious and you are about to be *so* free. Hope will come flooding back into your heart when you release that goodness without the requirement of return. You just release goodness because Jesus is in you, and He is goodness.

Today God is causing you to forget the wrongs, the injustice in your marriage, and He is healing your heart of the past. There may be some more new wrongs today, but you will be handling them differently moving forward. For now, let them go as you drift off to sleep, and in the morning you will have a brand new batch of mercy ready to go. Your goodness to your spouse is going to position them to transform, and position your marriage to succeed.

Can you imagine what would happen if today, right now, you just gave the past to Jesus?

"Here Jesus, you took this on the cross, I let go of it now."

I mean, you're reading a book designed to get things on the right track, you can see the light at the end of the tunnel, right? So why bring baggage with you on this journey? It is just so much easier to let the reset happen. Renew. Like that first day you met. Like your wedding day. When you get born again the Lord says to let go of the old self, He says "Behold, all things become new." This is how to renew your marriage. It's all new. You left for work today worried your marriage might be over. You got home thinking that you just aren't happy. But now, something is changing. In this moment, you are starting over. You are rebooting. There is no need to drudge up the past, since you can't even remember it. There isn't anything to work out or talk through. Now you are staring in the face of a bright future. Your marriage is made new in the language of your memory. Your new language can't remember wrongs. Old things have passed away. Listen, if this is how the Creator of heaven and earth works with us, then we know that it is the right way.

Chapter Three

The Secret Language of Kindness

"It is the small kindnesses done habitually that help keep a
relationship rich with love and respect."
Dennis Burke – Married since June 23, 1973

When Jesus was asked about marriage and divorce He said
this:

> Mark 10:6-9 (NKJV) [6] "But from the beginning of the
> creation, God ['made them male and female.'] [7] ['For
> this reason a man shall leave his father and mother
> and be joined to his wife,] [8] ['and the two shall
> become one flesh']; so then they are no longer two,
> but one flesh. [9] "Therefore what God has joined
> together, let not man separate."

Marriage is a coming together of two completely separate
people. It is uniting two into one. I want to discuss over the
next few chapters what it looks like to come together Spirit,
Soul and Body. We will begin with the soul in this chapter.
Here Jesus said "the two shall become…" This gives us the

37

idea of a process that takes place along a time table. The two are being drawn together and will become one. How long does this take? I'm certain it is different for every couple, but it would start with bringing the two closer. That makes sense, the two of you started in completely different locations when you were each born. Look how God has already been working to draw you together. Think about how the Lord had to work to get you both in the same place at the exact right moment in order for the sparks to fly. He has been drawing you together for a while.

Principle 4: Dare to speak the language of kindness.

Jeremiah 31:3 (NKJV) says "...with lovingkindness I have drawn you near." God shares with us the secret to the coming together we desire in our marriages. His lovingkindness draws us near. It doesn't push us. It doesn't compel us. It draws us. It isn't His love alone drawing us near, it is the expression of that love through kindness. Kindness draws us near. This is God's desire for your marriage. The two are becoming one through the drawing closer of each finding time to express lovingkindness. When we are expressing kindness to each other's soul, spirit, and body there is a drawing closer that makes us inseparable. It is truly allowing God to "join" us together. And what God joins together let no one put asunder.

A couple starts dating and the magnetic pull is felt. Two planets are thrust into each other's gravitational pull. It's like free-falling into each other's worlds. The man thinks about her day and night. She tells her friends, "I met someone!" I have found the *falling in love* is easy, not work. The relationship was in acceleration! Think about the role kindness was playing. After a year of marriage or so kindness is replaced with, well, maybe snippiness. Is that a word? We snip about a cup being left out. We snip. If kindness is drawing us near, then rudeness is pushing away. Something as simple as reconnecting to kindness today will have an eternal, supernatural impact in your home.

"It's impossible to be kind when he is always so distant, so rude." Yeah, I know, but draw upon HIS kindness. Jesus has plenty to go around, and it just didn't matter if someone rejected him or not. Jesus in you is kind. Kindness defeats rudeness. Kindness will win over time. As we discuss in the next three chapters the loving of the soul, the spirit, and the body, know that it is the secret language of kindness that will be pulling you both together.

This drawing together is for all three of the components that are "us". That is, we are a spirit, we have a soul, and we live in a body. Let me begin with the soul.

> Song of Solomon 3:4 King James Version (KJV) [4] It was but a little that I passed from them, but I found him whom my soul loveth: I held him, and would not let him go, until I had brought him into my mother's house, and into the chamber of her that conceived me.

"Whom my soul loveth..." This phrase is used many times in Song of Songs. It is Solomon and his loving bride, and a torrid love affair at that. It's interesting. She is expressing not just her love for him, but specifically, "My soul loves this man." The soul is the vault that holds your mind, your will, and your emotions. She is saying *my thoughts, my choices, and my emotions are in love with my lover*. The soul is the home for your feelings, philosophies, humor, dreams, personality, opinions, desires, worth, value, unworthiness, shame, hidden things, insecurities, past, scars, pain, decisions; really it is the sum of emotional and logical things that are unique to you.

Principle 5: Love your spouse with your soul.

You love with your soul in how you see her, what you say *to* her, and *about* her. This is a new language for your eyes and your lips. Loving your spouse with your thoughts and words will stir a new emotion and empower better choices.

Look in this Scripture how she is seeing and talking about her lover, loving him with thoughts and words.

> Song of Songs 1:3 (NKJV) [3] Because of the fragrance of your good ointments, Your name is ointment poured forth; Therefore the virgins love you.

In this verse the woman is saying, "Your name is smelly, but it's a good smell. And all the single chicks are smelling it too." A woman wants a man with a good name. Think of your name as the title that identifies you uniquely. It represents those unique characteristics that are your make up. The good, the bad, and the ugly. She is loving his uniqueness, and speaking highly of it. Our name is a big deal. The name of Jesus is a big deal. His name represents who He is, what He has done, and what He will do. His name is power. Faith in His name moves mountains. She is showing faith in the name of her lover. Loving the soul is loving and believing in all the unique things of your lover. All of them.

Think about the single life. (For just a second!) You meet someone and are interested, initially, because there is a physical attraction (maybe based on inward qualities).

"Okay, so yeah, you look good." And the pursuit begins from the foundation, or starting line of "I'm attracted." So stage one is "Yeah you look good…"

Stage two is "Now let's see the inside…" This is what the Bible is talking about, since "your name" is that unique identifier of who you really are. The soul is an eternal entity, just like the spirit. Your soul goes with you into eternity when you die. Not your body. So we date to figure out who we are dating. Break ups often happen because the "name" wasn't a good fit for us.

Some women even imagine or write down their name with his last name, "Hmm, Daphne Mcreyson would become, oh jeez, no, Daphne McDuck. NOOOOOOOOOO!"

Remember when you first started dating your spouse? You were attracted. Next, you begin to spend time together. And what happens? We start to share. Initially just the good stuff. As time goes on in the process some anger creeps out, or some mistakes. The past shames or guilts might come out as if to say, "There are things you should know about me before this goes any further. I'm from another planet." Well maybe not that. What is happening is we are looking for someone who will accept us, even the darker parts.

Opposites attract. We need to deal with this truth for a second. I will say it again in coming chapters. You found someone who doesn't think like you, or like what you like. My wife likes to hike. I like TV. My wife likes tuna fish on rye. My worst two hated foods in the world are tuna fish and rye bread. I think putting them together manifests one of the circles of hell. I like to cuddle when I sleep. She will cuddle and then move away to sleep. She says I'm "too hot". I don't think she means it the way I think of her hotness. One of the craziest ongoing fights of our lives has been that her number one most important sacred untouchable for our family is developing memorable moments through time together. She loves to vacation. I love to work. No, I cannot even begin to describe my need to be productive. Taking three days off of work in a row is impossible for me. One day off is plenty, I call it the Sabbath. Then it is back to work. It's a big one for me. Say it with me: "Cats and dogs!" You get the idea.

The opposing forces are designed to attract us together, not drive us apart. Dating websites that put people together based on common qualities are broken. They are perfect for making people into great friends, but where is the spark? Where is the passion in that? I want Han Solo and Princess Leia fighting right up to the moment that they kiss! Yeah. Opposites attract. And so did you. But now on to the problem at hand. You were attracted, but now those opposing forces threaten to drive you apart.

When you decided to get married you took a risk that you could survive the differences between you. But then some of you found after marriage that even more differences appeared. "Jeez, I knew I had to fix him some, but this is more than I expected. I better make a list!"

And so we try and fix each other. We accept their inside flaws but maybe with the idea we can fix them later. This is where the problem gets in. We begin to criticize and fault-find. Men begin to feel dumb and unwanted. Wives begin to feel worthless. A man's ego needs some food. A woman needs to be treasured.

In fact, let's face that for just a moment. What do we all want out of this life? What one thing is the most important of all things that we desire? Ultimately, from the time you are born, the BIG ONE we all need is to be loved EXACTLY as we are. It is the confusing misunderstood phrase "unconditional love." *Will you love me with no condition attached?*

"You see this big hot mess of a person full of baggage and flaws, but also full of dreams and desires, all of this (you motion to all of you), can you love this right now as it is?" God has tapped this desire in you and won you through it. Love is this, not that you loved God, but that He loved you, and gave... This is the ultimate desire we have.

Principle 6: Love is a river, not a cup.

Can you love their soul without the need to change it? Can you love your spouse's soul without the requirement of return? God's love is not a two way street. He just loves you without requiring you to love Him back. Interesting enough though, we do love Him because He first loved us. So this is the kind of love that actually works. Now then, what if you become a source of that love for your spouse? You draw on God's love for you and let it flow to them. Imitate God in how He loves.

I know a man who did just this. He married a girl who he knew was a gift from God. She came from brokenness and carried insecurity, fear, and a host of other wounds in her heart. He wasn't the perfect husband by any means. I got involved because she wanted a divorce. It was easy to see she was self-destructing. She was breaking the marriage before the marriage had a chance to break her. What I mean is, all she knew from family is that eventually those you love leave. So she had a self-defense system of leaving first. She was doing things to push her husband away. She was doing things many men would have left long ago for doing. But he kept saying to her, "I don't care about those things. I'm not leaving you. I love you." She literally was doing everything you can think of to destroy that love. It was as though she were testing him by saying, "Do you really love me unconditionally?? Is that even possible?" It was broken and dysfunctional behavior. Still, this man loved her as she was. All of her. I believe it was around the fourth year of their marriage that healing began to take place in her. I commend this man for loving her so deeply. I've seen many men just leave, and they were justified in leaving. In this case, I saw unconditional love heal and break generations of brokenness off of a family. She just needed to know she was loved and safe. His love was a river.

You and your spouse both need a place where you are loved exactly as you are. "Change nothing, ever, and I'll love you the same."

"But I have to make him into what I want!" No. You already decided that he is what you want. Now want him exactly as he is and he will be free to transform and grow. We resist change when we are rejected for our faults.

After accepting ALL of your spouse, you next need to embrace the differences. There are differences that Jesus will grow each of you out of, the differences that are dragged like old suit cases into our new lives from our former empty way of living in which we followed the flesh and its desires. Now you are being transformed by Christ. Your temper, or anxiety, or love of gossip, or name some other third thing, will fall off of you in time as Jesus does what Jesus does. I'm not talking about embracing the differences that need to go, and yet we still accept them exactly as they are! There are differences in you and your spouse that are part of your soul's unique design by God. These differences are part of why God welded you together.

For example, take my wife and me. I like to work. She loves to play. These are deep core values we each hold. A core value is a unique significant value in you that rips at your soul when violated. Investing time for memories with family is a sacred holy temple in my wife's heart. It is how God built her. On the other end of that same spectrum I hold sacred my need to produce. These two sacred core values are at complete odds with each other. After our first child turned one she wanted me to take two weeks off of work. She wanted to make memories. She was building a treasure trove of memories she could open later as the children grow up and move out.

"Can you take two weeks off of work?" You would think she had asked me to sever a limb. I conceded to one week. Then each day I would be on my email and phone telling her it was super important. The problem is that what was sacred to her, I kept violating. What was sacred to me she was stealing. These were some serious gut wrenching fights and stresses on the fabric of our relationship. The same may be happening in your marriage. A core value you hold may be under attack. Actually, it probably is. God has ordained this for many reasons, two of which I will share.

Many of us think love is a bank where you must make deposits in my account so that I can give back. This kind of love is lack mentality. This kind of love will leave you in a love famine. We say, "I will love you, but first, you should know, my love cup is running on low. I have nothing in my cup to give." This is conditional love by its very definition. In the Kingdom of God, love is a river that flows from God. I receive my value and love from God and then direct that river of love, which will never run dry, toward my spouse. Sometimes this love requires me to die a little bit to my own desires and dreams. Sometimes it may be a little bit like *a crucifying* of what I want. And so you are married. I hope your spouse isn't trying to crucify you, but certainly you can let one of your core values take a hit in order to fill up your spouse. In this is God's hidden gem. Romans Chapter 8 explains that we share in Christ's sufferings so that we may also share in His glory. In other words, sacrificial love of another person is the path through the cross, and to the glory! Now you share in glory. A glorious marriage.

My core value of work became an opportunity to show deep love to my wife. My unplugging from the job and making family memories my mission during vacation became a source of great sacrifice of my own life to her. She felt it. She really was #1. And the harvest, oh, the sweet harvest. Suddenly she was saying, "If you need to spend a couple of hours working in the morning it's fine. Do it." That was big. I realized a small part of her died in order to let me have that. I was loved.

The differing values you have from your spouse are actually a benefit. Without her, my life may be littered with a neglected family in exchange for hard work. I too was a benefit to her. Without me, her life may have been an endless play date. Together we are better. God did this. Now we take nice long vacations every year. She lets me work in the mornings most days. I work from about 5am to 10am with a short coffee break spent in prayer and in her gaze. Then it's play time. She lets me have my work because she says, "You're better the rest of the day if you had some time working. You're less distracted." So, today we sit near the coast in California literally on our summer vacation. It is 8:00am. We just finished our coffee, and now she works with me, as we write this book.

The other day we were at a restaurant and I wanted salty and she wanted sweet. So I ordered the cinnamon roll waffles and she ordered a green chili omelet. I ate half of hers. She ate half of mine. It was magical. What's my point? You have to define the differences in your spouse as the strength that you needed your whole life. God ordained it as vital to the destination He has for you, a plan to give you success and a future. You may have the waffles, but you really do need those green chili eggs too!

Maybe you and your spouse fight about the money. You like to spend, and your spouse is a cheap skate. Quality? Value? Maybe one is frivolous, taking no thought, but the other is a total planner. One is creative, the other is practical. "Come down to earth! You're living in la la land!" "I could say day, you'd say night. Tell me it's black when I know that it's white." (Lyrics from an 80's song). These opposite core values when embraced by you become a driving force in the attraction between you and your spouse. If you can get this one right, get ready for some fire! He likes to watch sports. Maybe be his cheerleader. Put on the short skirt and saunter down next to him with some ice-cream. Embrace the sport side of his life. Find out how it works with your core values. Before you know it, he's standing outside the dressing room where you are trying on clothes, and he is telling you which outfit he loves the most.

Principle 7: The secret language that will elevate your spouse.

> Song of Songs 2:3-4(NET) [3]Like an apple tree among the trees of the forest, so is my beloved among the young men. I delight to sit in his shade, and his fruit is sweet to my taste. [4] He brought me into the banquet hall, and he looked at me lovingly.

Look at how she talks about him! Look at how he was looking at her. Husbands, let the unrelenting hunger of your eyes be fed by only her and watch what happens. Notice how in the Scripture she saw in his eyes not just a hunger of desire though, although this is helpful. She noted how there was an intimacy attached to his look. He looked at her "lovingly". He loved her soul with a look. He was captured. Smitten. There was some insider information he had on her that no one else in the room knew. An intimate moment happened when their eyes met. Husbands, this is still inside of you. To be captivated by her. It is why you chased her in the first place. Let her SEE your attention on her. When another woman enters the room the enemy may try and make your wife feel insecure about her own beauty. Show her that all other beauty pales in comparison to your love for her. Be intentional about communicating to your wife that there is no one (and nothing) you would rather look at than her. That gaze can mean so much to her. You are loving her soul. There may be a million people in the room, but your eyes are on your prize!

Let's take this a bit deeper. The Lord tells us we will gain His promises if we can first see them.

> 2 Corinthians 5:7 (KJV) [7]For we walk by faith, not by sight:)

Paul writes in Romans 4:16 (NIV) "Therefore, the promise comes by faith..." We may see sickness, but we don't walk by what we see, we walk by faith. Jesus has provided healing on the cross. In other words, the best of God comes to us when we can spiritually see and believe the unseen things that He has freely given us at the cross. The Lord tells us often in the Bible to "lift up our eyes and see."

> Genesis 13:14-15 (NKJV) [14] And the LORD said to Abram, after Lot had separated from him: "Lift your eyes now and look from the place where you are-- northward, southward, eastward, and westward; [15] "for all the land which you see I give to you and your descendants forever..."

Now, how does this tie back to how you look at your spouse? Well, how do you see them? Do you see their faults or their potential? How was he seeing her?

Realize that looking lovingly at your spouse calls the best out of them. The hidden things in them become visible when you learn to see what may be hidden. Consider just a simple worldly example: A woman gets dressed up and cares for her appearance, but her husband is distracted. She is hurt. He didn't even notice. What happens next? Well, why should she try to look nice? She stops fixing herself up. It is the same for husbands. How she looks at him will call him higher or send him crashing.

How you see someone will determine what you receive from them.

Consider those in Jesus home town who only saw a carpenter. The Bible says that *Jesus could do few healing and miracles* there. Did they need miracles? Yes. But they could not receive from Him because of how they saw Him. How you see your spouse will greatly impact what you receive from them. If you see him as a loser, he will become one. He may fight it for a while but eventually you will get what you see. How do you see your wife? Do you see her as valuable? Do you see her as strong and courageous? Do you see her rich in kindness? Maybe she isn't kind all the time. But don't see what you have, see what you know is in her. See her as beautiful, strong, valuable, smart, loving, for she will become what you see. You will only receive from her how you see her.

Looking at the Scripture in Song of Songs again:

> Song of Songs 2:3-4(NET) [3]Like an apple tree among the trees of the forest, so is my beloved among the young men. I delight to sit in his shade, and his fruit is sweet to my taste. [4] He brought me into the banquet hall, and he looked at me lovingly.

Listen to how she speaks of him. "Like an apple tree among trees of the forest..." She didn't call him a Microsoft tree, unstable, always crashing. He was an apple tree. (I'm having fun now)

She is saying, "He stands out. He has the fruit I want. He is producing. He is tall in stature and unique." Now I'm not very tall in stature, but I like it when my spouse talks about me this way. She can't really call me a tree, but she says I'm a *shrub among the shrubs; a crab apple shrub.* I'm okay with that.

In today's society it's just way too common for spouses to speak ill of each other when away from each other's company, complaining to friends or mom about the inadequacies. "Ugh, she just makes me so mad! She makes no sense!" The world has developed a habit of forming alliances outside of our marriage that are in opposition to each other.

Loving your spouse's soul isn't just done with a gaze, but also with words. She wasn't addressing his physical appearance, although that is good too. She was talking up his soul. She loves to rest in the safety of his arms. He is a great provider and protector, nay, not just great, the greatest. She loves just to sit near him. She knows the other women would be lucky to have him. You may be saying, "I have nothing good to say right now." We don't only see what we want, we say what we want. Isn't this also how our relationship with God works? Our words are powerful, they carry the power of life and death in them. In other words, we get what we say.

> Romans 4:17 King James Version (KJV) [17] ...even God, who quickeneth the dead, and calleth those things which be not as though they were.

We often describe our problems instead of calling things higher. Why not say out loud who you desire her to be? Say it as though it is already done. Maybe your spouse is a dead-beat, non-working, church-hating fuddy duddy. (Not sure where the fuddy duddy came from.) Call him a successful, family-loving, hard working, church going, best husband ever. He's a tall apple tree. He may even know you're not being realistic, but he is listening. Your words have power. See, you love her exactly as she is, but then you call her higher through building her up. Ephesians chapter five teaches us we have authority over each other's bodies as a married couple. Paul tells us a few times in the New Testament that he doesn't use his authority to tear down, but to build up. Use your authority to speak success into your spouse's future. How you talk about your spouse matters. And in this Scripture we get the idea that she wasn't talking to him, but instead she was talking to others about him. I don't think he was even nearby.

Imagine just for a moment you walk into your bedroom and you can hear a quiet conversation coming from the closet, you can't make out the words but your husband is on his phone. You creep closer to the closed door and lean in cautiously, "Who is he talking to, and what about?" You wonder. Then your ears start to form the mumbling into words. "My wife is so incredible. The thing is she is probably the smartest person I've ever met. No seriously, I'm an absolute mindless jerk sometimes and she just keeps pouring into this family, tireless..." This man is about to get lucky! His wife will burst into the closet, snatch the phone from his hands and it is ON! This is loving the soul loud and clear.

We really do believe what others say about us. How much more do we believe what our spouse says about us? The message you convey to your spouse about who you think they are is who they will believe they are. It is who they will reflect and ultimately who they will become.

Remember Jesus healing a crippled man? He didn't say, "You are a sinner and I can't help you until you become a better person." No, He loved people exactly as they were. To one He said, "Your sins are forgiven you." This man didn't even ask for forgiveness. Jesus didn't just describe the person's problem either. He didn't say, "Boy, are you crippled." So often we approach our relationships the way the world has taught us. We tell people what is wrong with them, we tell others what is wrong with them, and then, if they change, we might accept them. Jesus accepted them first. Then he spoke a different message about them, which in turn, called them higher. It is the same for your spouse. Love them exactly as they are. Speak a different word about them. Those words are calling them higher. In any *other* scenario the blind man would not see. But in Jesus' system, the blind man will be able to do things he could never do. To the crippled man He said, "Get up, take your mat and walk." He called the cripple man to accomplish something no one else believed he was capable of. It is the same for you and your spouse. In a marriage our words and how we see each other will bring us higher, or conversely, will send us spiraling downward.

Don't just get caught looking lovingly at your spouse's soul. Get caught talking great about them. Let your kind words get back to him/her through a family member. Could it really be as simple as how you look and talk about your spouse? Yep. It could. God makes it so easy.

Remember this. Once I'm secure that my soul is loved exactly as I am, then you can call me higher. Calling me higher happens in how you see me and how you talk about me. My soul is loved as you love my name, that is, my whole soul. You are loving the way I think, the way I feel, the choices I make. In all, you are loving me without condition, you see me different than anyone else, you look at me different and it matters. You talk about me different too, which is calling me higher. You are loving my soul. In the next chapter we will open up about loving the spirit. Are you ready?

Chapter Four
The Secret Language of the Spirit

"We wanted godly companions to share our lives with...We have always been faithful and active in church."
Dave and Louise Lindley - Married since October 24, 1970

Coming together as one isn't just about knitting our soul together, but also means a drawing together in spirit. Love her Spirit. Love his Spirit. Loving the Spirit within your spouse is accomplished through learning the language of the Spirit.

I asked a couple who has been married for 48 years the key to their happiness. They both said, without even thinking about it, that it was their daily prayer time. They would take long walks early in the morning and pray together: Spiritual things.

> 1 Corinthians 2:14 (KJV) [14]But the natural man receiveth not the things of the Spirit of God: for they are foolishness unto him: neither can he know them, because they are spiritually discerned.

The natural mind cannot understand the spiritual things, but the Spirit receives the things of the Spirit. Even though you're stuck in a clay pot world, full of stinky garbage disposals and leaky cars, you can engage in eternal things every day, feeding the spirit of each other.

Understand that as a Christian we have access to help that doesn't make sense. It is supernatural help. We can tap into God's anointing for our marriage. There may be no more impactful chapter than the chapter on loving your spouse's spirit. And to access the spiritual things we must take a chapter to look at God's Spiritual house! So let's get right into it.

You are a spirit. You were made in God's likeness and image, and God is Spirit. You have a soul. You live in a body. The spirit is you. You were born of Spirit. You are the offspring of God. You were born in the flesh as a baby, but when you received Jesus you were born again, born of Spirit.

So the core of who I really am is a spirit. Born of an incorruptible seed! The Spirit desires spiritual. So how do I love the spirit? Well, what does the spirit want? Jesus said, "My words are spirit and they are life." He also said, "Man does not live by bread alone but on every word that proceeds from the mouth of God." The Spirit wants spiritual things. The Spirit wants you to pay attention to what is spiritual and eternal. The Spirit loves the words of Jesus. The Word of God! This is our spiritual food. The food is in God's house.

When there is no hope, there is always hope with God. When things look impossible, they are possible in God's hands. This is spirit: Prayer, worship, and thanking God. The training center for spiritual things in your home and family is Gods house. There is spiritual food in God's house!

Later in this book we will look at the flesh desires. Consider flesh desires for a second. The flesh wants to eat. When you give it food it communicates fulfillment, a quite wonderful feeling. Ahhhh, food. MMMMMMM. How much deeper is the fulfillment experienced by the Spirit? Ahhhhhh. Imagine a spouse who is on board with God's destiny and purpose for your life. You see, destiny and purpose come from the anointing of God on your life, which is spiritual. Imagine the fulfillment. Our marriage needs to be actively engaged in this fulfillment.

> Ephesians 5:25 (NIV) [25]Husbands, love your wives, just as Christ loved the church and gave himself up for her.

Jesus died for the Church. Imagine the importance of His spiritual house in your world. It is designed to invade your home and feed your spirit. In this chapter I want to teach you how being in God's house as a couple will become a pillar of success in your marriage. The Church is a spiritual house full of spiritual food and spiritual promises.

God's house is a spiritual house full of spiritual food. Here you come once per week, you pray, you sing and make music in your heart to God, and you hear the life changing Word of God declared over your life. Loving your spouse's spirit means being in God's house.

> Acts 2:47 (NKJV) [47]...And the Lord added to the church daily those who were being saved.

In other words, God isn't just interested in getting people saved, His next step is to add them into the church. He was "adding them to the church."

> Luke 4:16 (NIV) [16](Jesus) went to Nazareth, where he had been brought up, and on the Sabbath day he went into the synagogue, *as was his custom.* He stood up to read...

The part of this passage I emphasized for you is that being in church once a week was a custom for Jesus. The same phrase is used later in the Bible for Paul. Once per week they went to church. "Did Jesus go to church?" Yes. And it wasn't a habit, or a tradition, it was a custom. A custom is deep. Like Thanksgiving, it isn't something you just skip. Jesus is in us. You know He is with you every day and everywhere. Do you know where He wants to go once-a-week though? Church. If you lived in Jesus' day and you wanted to hear him preach on the Sabbath, you would have to go to church. Keep in mind He didn't agree with the church He went to. In fact, the people in the church wanted to kill Him. But He still went.

For your marriage, weekly church is a wonderful benefit. It brings you into unity in spirit. God's house offers you rest and hope. It is the storehouse where the food you need is. Imagine a marriage where you and your spouse (and family) went to church, sat and prayed, worshipped God together, and heard the message while holding hands. A marriage where you tithed together, sowed some seed and believed God for that thing you have been praying for is moving in the right direction. How often? Once per week.

Principle 8: Immerse Yourself in the Secret Language of God.

God doesn't talk like others. Jesus didn't say things everyone else was saying. He came with a new language. His Word's hold all of creation together. It is a language that works. When we get around how He talks, it impacts how we talk. If you live in foreign country for a length of time you begin to pick up a new way to communicate. God's House is a new kingdom, and His language doesn't sound anything like the news or your co-workers. I love reading the Word of God, but it really is different when we hear it spoken! God's house is the right message we need every week, it is our bread, practical and useful. God's house is my supply for what I will need in the coming week. God's house is the place of peace, and we need to have a sanctuary in our lives, a retreat, a place of rest. God's house is the place where true transformation takes place, and each of us need that transformation in order to be set free of the old ways. God's house holds the pattern for a successful home and family, and His pattern can invade your home. In this chapter I will discuss these truths at length.

First, why be in God's house every week? Well *because He said so*. That answer doesn't always work. Think about the *message* of God's house. Hope. Love. Forgive. You can do it. Ponder those moments when you are singing and the Spirit of God wraps you up like a glove. Jesus inside of you is drawing you into God's house once per week. It is His custom. Search for a great church in your community that speaks to you. When it is right, the Spirit in you will say "YES, THIS ONE!"

> Ezekiel 47:12 (NIV) [12]Fruit trees of all kinds will grow on both banks of the river. Their leaves will not wither, nor will their fruit fail. Every month they will bear fruit, because the water from the sanctuary

flows to them. Their fruit will serve for food and their leaves for healing."

We are those fruit trees. This section of Ezekiel is a prophesy of the church Jesus established for us; He told Peter "Upon this rock I will build my church and the gates of hell cannot stand against it." Church is the only entity on the planet that Jesus said could crush the gates of hell. Here the fruit trees are fruitful. The identifying source of that fruit is "because the water from the sanctuary flows to them." Church. God's house speaks a different language than the world. We need a different language.

Principle 9: Have the right priorities.

My Dad is a great man of God, a pastor, a general in the Christian army. He was already in ministry when I was ten years old. This means he was gone morning to evening. Full time ministry doesn't really have a break built into it, because, technically, you work even on the day everyone else is off and having church. One day my dad was driving me to a soccer game. He had a meeting at the church so he was dropping me off. At the half-time break of the game I saw my dad sitting in the grass watching me play. I ran to him. Something happened in my heart that day. I felt it and never forgot it. I asked, "What are you doing here?"

He paused, smiled, and said, "I'll never miss a game again because of ministry. You come first."

It may sound like he put me above God, but that isn't true. He placed his family above ministry. Me and my brother stayed in church. Most every minister's kid we knew growing up ran from God. Why? Because God stole their childhood. My dad never put us before God, but he did put his family before ministry. He placed his first church ahead of the church family. Just a little ahead, but ahead.

I remember a phone call one night, when we were having a family night playing games. Our family night was every Thursday night. My dad and mom were at church Wednesday night. Tuesday night was youth music rehearsal for my dad. Monday night he worked on cars. Friday night was his date night. The phone rang. All I know is that there was an emergency marriage meeting that had to take place that night, and they needed my dad. It had to be tonight! Tough decision. My dad handled it calmly. "I'm sorry, I can meet with you tomorrow at the office. Tonight is out of the question." Long pause as the other person spoke; we could hear the emotion and desperation. "Then tonight at 8:30pm we can talk over the phone. But now will not work." When he gets off the phone he says, "Remind me to not answer the phone when it's family night."

I never forgot it. Legacy with your kids will greatly depend on priority. Where do they fit? While other minister kids were literally hating God as they lost their parents, we were seeing the benefits of ministry and family. Most pastor kids of that generation did not follow in their parents footsteps. My brother and I did. This is because my parents didn't abandon their family for ministry. Ministry had a powerful place in our life, but family was just above it.

Now, today, it is quite often I'm asked, "How come you weren't at the meeting on Wednesday night, it was a powerful message?" My response is, "There is a powerful meeting here almost every night of the week, but if I attend them all I will lose my family. And if I lose my family, I don't get to do this (ministry) anymore."

And so here is a good system for prioritizing your time:

1. God – Jesus – Holy Spirit
2. Immediate Family (Your first church)
3. Occupation - Business
4. Ministry (helping others)

Now sometimes you have to "work" on a family night. That's fine. The thing is, if you lose your job because you have put your family "first," well then, you can't really take care of your family. So a source of money is technically very much loving your family and putting your family above your own needs. In other words, a person doesn't work for themselves, but for the household benefit. So in one case you might have to work all weekend and miss the lake trip. It's okay. For this reason ministry has to be in the seat behind your work. Ministry has to be in the seat behind going to church. If you volunteer at the church five days a week but don't have a job, and keep missing service, you won't flourish as God intends.

Billy Graham talked about early ministry life, and how if he could go back and change just one thing, he would have spent more time with his children. He has just one regret. Don't let this be your regret. If the great Billy Graham is helping us rethink family and ministry, then we as the entire body of Christ need to do the same.

Now, this thinking has changed greatly in America. Ministers have learned about the priority of family and have abandoned the old religious and mistaken teaching of leaving your children for the sake of the Gospel. When Jesus told a man, "Anyone who puts his hand to the plow and then turns back is not worthy of the Kingdom work," He was addressing that you shouldn't start a family and then leave them. The plow here was that he had kids and a wife, and needed to finish that work. Do you understand?

If you are heavily drawn to ministry but have young children a great solution is for one to stay home with the kids while the other goes to the meeting or rehearsal. This is how my wife and I handled ministry, and I'm in it full time. We both are. But we were at the meeting and at home at the same time.

When I say *sit in the sanctuary* I am addressing both ministers and volunteers. Sometimes volunteers are so busy with classes and work at God's house, they forget to sit in the sanctuary. Soon the well is dry. The spiritual food is in the sanctuary. Classes are good, but God's system is clear. The food flows from the pulpit. His design. Don't just be "at church". Be "in church."

What about the seven day week? Six days you are out doing your thing and the world is trying to beat you down. The world's message is trying to tell you who you are, what you want, what you can or can't do. The world is trying to fill you with the wrong message. So God says to come to His house once per week, plant in that house, and listen to the words delivered in the sanctuary. It is water for you. Now you are fruitful. Think about fruit trees that aren't in proximity of that sanctuary water. Look at the promise you miss out on. A marriage planted in church is strong, hopeful, and united. It is a marriage that will bear fruit. You are putting your family in the stronghold, the fortress, Zion, the city who's architect and builder is the Lord.

Let's ponder the idea of the Sabbath. Once per week you do no work. No chores. Just go to church and then chill with your family. Now we know no one does the Sabbath anymore. Still, think about how it is in God's top ten list, right alongside of wisdom such as "don't murder." So think about the wisdom of working six days and resting one. That rest includes God's house. If we work all seven days, then we are so tired all the time we run out of gas with our work, our business, and our relationships. God knows how He can recharge you in just one day. We are way more productive the other six days if we can get our one day of rest. He can erase the pressures of the world and get you back to hoping and forgiving if you can just give Him one spiritual day. It really doesn't matter which day you choose as your Sabbath, but your marriage needs one. It needs a down day. A day to worship God, pray, hear the Word, and rest. No chores. No errands. Rest. Have a BBQ, watch some football, go to church. Rest! Be busy the other six days.

The Greek word used as "Church" when Jesus talked about His church is ἐκκλησία. It literally means (please google this for yourself!) "A gathering of citizens called out of their homes into some public place as an assembly." I think it's funny that Jesus made sure to pick a definition that eliminates the idea you can just have church at home. He wants you to gather with the other believers. Jesus was always gathering people, his team, together, and then he would feed them. This is for us. We need good strong trees growing around us.

In marriage, other strong marriages will bring strength to yours. In a church setting there will be plenty of marriages in tough spots, and plenty that are rocking. As you get to know these people, then more of what they are up to and makes their marriages work will get on both of you.

"I wish my husband treated me like that guy treats his wife."

Okay, well, remember the last chapter. Dare to speak a different language about your husband. But still, getting him around that man will probably help, and that is part of God's brilliance for church. We get around some people going the same way we are trying to go.

What if your spouse doesn't want to go to church? The answer is in the Bible; I'll paraphrase it in principle. First, don't fret about it. Live at peace in your homes. Be amazing. Be loving and encouraging. Show your spouse what Jesus looks like. Second, in a loving way, sell going to church. Sell it. Pair it with something they like to do. "Hey honey, how about on Sunday we go to church and then (something they love to do)." Or "If there were one thing I would ask, and I know you don't like to do this, but just one request, in fact, do nothing else for me if you like, but come to church with me. Sit and hold my hand." Sell it. Reward it. Remember, just positioning them for transformation can be enough. Let Jesus do the rest. Remember, you are partnering with God on this one. He wins! "The lost one is sanctified by the saved one." You're the saved one. Jesus is going to win!

We all need a safe place to return to!

> Psalms 76:2-3 (NIV) [2] His tent is in Salem, his dwelling place in Zion. [3] There he broke the flashing arrows, the shields and the swords, the weapons of war.

Salem means peace, and by "tent" He is referring to your body. Moses built God a tent of meeting, which was God's house on the move. They could pack it up and go place to place. It was church in a suit case. Much later, King Solomon built a temple for the Lord. The tent represents you and your family. The Spirit of God is in you, which is God on the move.

Jesus has made you his tent. When you received Him you became the tent of peace. What I'm saying is that Jesus is *in* your family. He has made your family a place anointed for peace. Jesus is the Prince of Peace. So your home and family is anointed supernaturally for peace, a place absent of storms.

God says here that He is also dwelling in Zion. This is the temple Solomon built. It is the church. Zion is God's house. Both places are places of family.

Have you ever gone tent camping? We pack up all the food and supplies we will need for our tent before we leave. You get out your cooler, get into the pantry and fridge and make sandwiches. God calls His house the "storehouse". Your home and family are represented by the tent. We go to His house to prepare our tent with the supplies we need for camping this week. We may need fire, food, blankets, water, or whatever for our family. In this case we receive all the supply from the store house.

Then He anoints it for peace, because the world is a place of battle. We go to work and battle. School is a battle. We are out and about taking territory. A successful army sets up base, a safe place to restock and get rested to go out on the next mission.

When you plant your marriage in God's house you step into this anointing for peace in your home and in your church. If the world is a place for battle and the home and the church are anointed for peace, why is it that most of the battles are happening in the home and at church? Think about it. Where do most of the battles in life seem to happen? Family. The reason is that Satan knows if your home becomes what it purposed for, a sanctuary of rest and recharge that you will begin to take territory. When the Israelites were taking territory in the Promised Land they set up base camp in Gilgal. After every battle they would return to Gilgal. This was the place of the covenant, which is reminder of the family of God that has been provided in Christ Jesus. They needed a place to recharge before going out to take more territory. This is why Satan works so hard to make our tent and our temple a place of war. But the truth today brings freedom. Today that is breaking off of your life. The anointing is breaking the bonds and the yoke that have been on your life. Your home is becoming a place of peace and God himself is breaking the weapons of war off of your household.

When the home is a battleground everyone in the family has to find some other place to escape to. When the home becomes what it is anointed to be, a place of peace, then everyone huddles and recharges as they ready to take new territory. This means we win a lot more, too, since we are rested. When God's House is your supply center it is because your family has planted in the stronghold and you are safe. God is your canopy of protection. You are dwelling in the secret place of the Most High. Look again at what the Scripture says. "There he broke the flashing arrows, the shields and the swords, the weapons of war." Jesus broke the weapons of war off your house. When you step into this Scripture all the drama leaves, and your home becomes a place you run to after the battles of normal life. Your church is a place you run to in times of trial. This is how Jesus dwells (or rolls).

Interestingly enough, Satan attacks the idea of church and family as often as possible. He is scared to death at what will happen to your family if you plant in God's House. He will do everything he can to get your feelings hurt at church. He wants to bring confusion at church. He wants you nitpicking and fighting at home. He wants husbands to have to stop at the bar because going home just means more fighting. *At the bar no one judges him.*

The city of Jerusalem represents the church. The name means "city of peace." Historically the city of Jerusalem has been attacked, under siege, and conquered more than any other city in history. In other words, the greatest attack from Satan is going to be to keep you out of your city of peace, the church! Satan does not like the church. It is the one thing that his gates cannot stand against! If you want to push him way out of your family, position your family in God's house.

God's House is the house of transformation. It's true. As you love your spouse exactly as they are, your fear may be that they will never grow. *Will she ever change? Will he stop with the anger?!* But real growing happens as a result of God's Word invading our soul and showing us Who Christ is.

Transformation is what Jesus does best. Maybe the pastor is speaking on anger this week. Wouldn't you know it, you have been praying about anger. Man, it's in your house. Aren't you glad you have your family in church this week? Now while the Word is being preached don't look at your spouse repeatedly, and NO NUDGING! Someone else is going to use the Word of God to say what you have been thinking! As the pastor speaks the Word of God, the Holy Spirit starts to perform surgery. Supernatural healing takes place. Anger is being broken off of you and your family. Your dad had it. His dad had it. But you just got free of it. Now your kids are free too. This is Jesus breaking the arrows and the weapons of war. He does it. We just position ourselves to hear it.

Later that week you are having your weekly meeting with your spouse. The two of you thank God for delivering you all of anger. You pray for your children. You pray about the bills. You were feeling a bit overwhelmed, but now you are hopeful. You are energized. Lovingkindness has replaced criticisms and anger. There is praise and worship music playing. You look at the goals that seem too big but then you remember how far God has brought you. "God is bigger," you say as you pull out of the driveway and head into another week. Feed that spirit. Feed it. Give it prayer. Give it the Bible. Position it in God's House.

I know a man who was addicted to marijuana. The addiction had stolen his ambition to win in life. He would sit at home and do nothing while his wife tried to make ends meet for her and the kids. She was in church every weekend praying for him. One day she found a way to get him to start coming to church with her. I don't know what she did, but there he was. Now I know this man all these years later, and he tells me that he would get high before he came. He told me that he was high every Sunday at church for a year. There was no change. But then one Sunday morning the power of God hit him during the message. He received Jesus that day and was completely and supernaturally delivered of his addiction. He is now back to work and highly successful. The wife couldn't nag him out of his addiction, but she could drag him to the house of the God who would set him free. She got him to Zion. She moved him to the mountain of the Lord's inheritance to get stocked up on the peace his tent truly needed, not peace from pot, but the peace of God.

God's House doesn't just transform you and your spouse through the water of the sanctuary, that life-giving spoken Word of God taught by His Holy Spirit, but God's House will transform your whole family. It is the spiritual food that will take your family to supernatural heights! God's House is the pattern for your house. His dwelling is the pattern for your tent. When Moses set out to build the Tabernacle (tent) for the Lord God told him to "carefully follow the pattern I will show you." In Hebrews we find out that the pattern was following the Spiritual House in heaven, Zion. In other words, your tent, your home and family, is designed to follow the pattern of God's house carefully. The Church is a family. God's House is the family training center. God shows you how to be a great father. Jesus is your brother and groom. He calls us all brothers and sisters.

No matter how crazy your home was when you grew up, God can reprogram you with His House. We naturally follow the pattern of the home we grew up in. Your marriage is currently impacted by how each of you watched your parents in their relationship. The pattern you saw is impacting your marriage now, either because you rejected that pattern or because you fell into it. God has a new pattern for you to follow. A perfect pattern. As you go to the storehouse the ways of that house will naturally become an image in your home. The food in God's House begins to stock your family pantry. "Oh you need some hope. Funny, we just picked some up on Sunday; let me grab it off of the shelf." As you pray openly in church, it will slowly find its way into your house. As you worship you find yourself worshipping at home. You were thankful to God in a tough time, and suddenly you're being thankfully to God at home. The pastor spoke such an interesting word on Sunday that your husband is reading the Bible investigating and learning for himself. *Who is this man?* God's House is invading your house. Your son is sick and you find yourself saying, "Let's pray. Let's lay hands on the sick and they SHALL RECOVER!" Oh it's about to get real in this place!

The relationship drama we experience in church is all part of God's plan. That probably sounds funny, but He is a God that knows us. He knew when He put us all together in the same church that we would fight some. When leaving is no longer an option, personal growth is the only solution.

Proverbs 17:17 (KJV) [17]A friend loveth at all times, and a brother is born for adversity

In church God gave you brothers. A brother is there to fight with you. They are born to make you stronger. Think about this, God literally placed a person in your life at church to pick a fight with you. Why?

In church we are learning how to love better. In order to remain in church, you have to. It's true. In God's house there are people. People can create drama. We are brothers and sisters. A "brother is born for adversity." Wait, we are all brothers and sisters born after our Jesus (the first born of many brothers and sisters). Brothers and sisters in church are going to battle sometimes. Satan wants drama in God's house. People get hurt in church. It's actually part of God's system though. It is part of his training and pattern.

Philippians 3:10-11 (NIV) [10] I want to know Christ--yes, to know the power of his resurrection and participation in his sufferings, becoming like him in his death, [11] and so, somehow, attaining to the resurrection from the dead.

We have all seen before that sometimes people leave family when adversity strikes. But a brother is born for adversity. A puppy battles and gnaws on another puppy, and through it they both get tougher. One puppy doesn't say, "That's it! You nicked my ear. I'm finding another puppy litter." (A puppy can't actually talk).

It is in the staying and remaining that we grow. We learn to be more forgiving, and more loving. The Bible often tells us to participate in the sufferings of Christ. This always has bothered me, as I wonder, what does that mean? Does that mean God wants me to be sick? NO! The SUFFERINGS of Christ we are asked to participate in is simply resisting temptation and loving people even when they are impossible to love. Christ wasn't sick or something. That wasn't his suffering. Did he have a disease? No. Did he go to minister in Galilee but ran out of money and had to file for bankruptcy? No. What were His sufferings? Jesus sufferings were the people. People are the "fellowship of suffering" we join with Christ. I'm not a big suffering kind of guy and I don't agree at all that God does anything to me that would hurt me or take life from me. No, Christ's sufferings didn't even come from Satan. Satan could do nothing to Jesus. Christ's sufferings were people. The same people He loved were mean to him. The same guy he healed of leprosy was shouting "Crucify Him!" *Gee. Thanks bro.* You will deal with some of the same. These people are at your work. They are your neighbors. They are your family. They are in your church. They watch CNN or FOX news. This is our drama. Your quest, should you choose to accept it, is one where you care about others more than yourself. It is an adventure where you love the unlovable, you become the safe place everyone so desires, and you become the voice of value in a world that is in a value famine. It really is a completely different language.

Christ's only suffering was people rejecting him, hating him, insulting him. His response? Love and forgiveness. Does He win? Yes. And we are being transformed more and more into His likeness. Romans 8 tells us we are joint heirs with Christ, "if indeed we share in His sufferings so that we may also share in His glory." So Paul says, "I rejoice in my sufferings..." He's like, "People being mean to me? Bring IT! It literally makes me better. I have gains!" In others words, the more I remain in God's House despite the drama, the more I forgive unconditionally the people who have hurt my feelings, betrayed what I know to be right, and grieved my soul, the more Christ has gains in me. Parts of me are dying that Christ is resurrecting! My job is to forgive and love! The result? *Now I see supernatural resurrection power in my life.* Resurrection power has no effect if something hasn't died. So when people dislike you and say hurtful things about you, when your brothers and sisters wrong you, but you just forgive em and keep loving, you die a little more, and so you grow. Further, you are ushering peace into that place. **And this will invade your home.** What is happening? The "weapons of war" are being broken, and you are literally becoming a source of unlimited peace as Christ makes huge gains in your spirit.

> Colossians 3:13-14 (NIV) [13] Bear with each other and forgive one another if any of you has a grievance against someone. Forgive as the Lord forgave you. [14] And over all these virtues put on love, which binds them all together in perfect unity.

This was a Word for the church, among the brothers and sisters. Are there going to be grievances? Yes! And what are we told to do with them? Forgive and love anyways. This pattern will invade your house. Now sometimes we move to another church home because God has a new revelation to get into you, and the home you are in is missing something critical like God's grace, faith, Spirit, or has left sound doctrine. Or maybe you moved out of state. But if it's adversity or hurt or persecution, man, get ready to be a remainer. This pattern means adversity will no longer divide your tent, that is, your home and family. Do you see God's brilliance here?

When my brother (real life brother not church brother) hurts my feelings, he doesn't stop being my brother. I don't leave and find a new family. But in the world, families are being broken apart. When we plant in the church, we position ourselves to have that pattern broken off of our lives. Family stays together and loves no matter what. This pattern should be established in God's house, and then lived out in your home.

Jesus spoke of loving the way He loves, which means laying down your life for each other. Love is giving up what we hold most dear for someone else with no expectation of returned favor. It lays down your life. This is the line we all got in. It is the Jesus line. It's becoming life for someone else at the expense of crushing your own bones. In this we gain Christ. Literally. My flesh becomes lesser so that Christ becomes greater in me. I'm letting Jesus have expression in my life. He is love. In this, I become more Christ-like. I am "sharing in His suffering so that I might also share in His glory." Jesus has packaged a promised blessing in the unfair persecution, insults, and hate that you endure. "Blessed are you when people persecute you, insult you..." It was one of his first teachings in Matthew chapter five. He didn't say people wouldn't be hard to love, He said that if we respond with forgiveness toward the unlovable, there is a hidden blessing inside, and that benefit is far greater than the cost.

A whole chapter devoted to feeding the spirit? I wish it were the whole book. God's House is our supply house, our house of peace, our house of transformation, and our reprogramming center for our family. Take a day once per week, feed and love the spirit of your spouse.

Chapter Five

Speak the Language of Passion

"At the age of 45 I was blessed to reconnect with and marry my childhood sweetheart. Twenty-two years later we remain the truest of sweethearts. All I can say is: *Thank you Lord for Heaven on earth!*"

Debbie Moore - Married since December 31, 1995

Not only do we speak a new language to the soul, and to the spirit, but we are learning to speak the language of passion.

The language of passion is a forgotten language in the home. Sometimes it is forgotten because of cultural influence. We have been programmed that the fire always wanes as a relationship grows. That is a lie meant to deceive you and steal your joy. Why would the heat of romance be reserved for a short term relationship? It doesn't even make sense. It certainly isn't God's plan for you.

The language of passion is forgotten sometimes because of a person's agenda. In the limited time given to accomplish the tasks of life, and especially once you have children, speaking the language of passion is swept into the corners of our calendars until one day we are so hungry for something hotter and spontaneous we find ourselves unhappy. Yet, the passion can be kindled right in your own home. How? By simply re-engaging with speaking that language to your spouse. It really is that easy.

The language of passion is necessary to renew your spark into a roaring flame. This language is oil for your spark. It is fire wood designed for a nice long burn. It is spoken through affection. It is also communicated in pursuit (more on this later). Third, it is the declaration of your spouse's beauty. (We know you think she's pretty, but why not tell her.) Last, it is learning to understand your spouse's body, that is, what gets their motor started…so to speak.

News flash – affection and making love are both God's invention. In this chapter I want to talk about the language of passion. We will be learning that daring to speak the language of passion will be reigniting the romance that may seem to some just a distant memory. God desires to stoke the fire of the flame you have for one another, and to make that flame relentless.

Intimacy and sex is something you have wanted since you hit puberty. Under the umbrella of marriage God is saying "Yeah, go get it!" Come taste and see that the Lord is good!

As Christians can we decide right now to take back affection and sex? Can we decide Satan does not own the real estate on making love? We watch the movies and see the affection of two, kissing goodbye with that warmth and deep desire we all want. Listen, what the world shows us will pale in comparison to the smoldering romance God wants for you. To be honest, the world doesn't even know what they are doing. Christians are literally armed and dressed to be better at everything. The world may have 50 shades of gray, but we have 51,000 shades of pure unadulterated crazy!

Principle 10: The Forgotten Language of Affection.

Affection is one of the big contrasting additions you have with each other that sets you far and above a friendship. Affection is a form of communication. It is a language. You are lovers. You are affectionate. You can speak a great deal of words without even talking when you understand the language of affection. You could be having dinner with a group of friends, but on the way to dinner you and your spouse had a big fight. (Fights seem to happen at the worst times, right?) There is all of this tension between you as you try and get through the night with a smile. But then you let it go. You place your hand on her hand, and give her that goofy smile that says you are sorry and you don't want to fight anymore. Not a word was said, and yet, you said a million things with a simple touch.

> Song of Songs 1:2 (NET) [2] Oh, how I wish you would kiss me passionately! For your lovemaking is more delightful than wine.

Have we stopped kissing? She talks about kissing in this verse. Bring kissing back. Find yourself kissing in places where you can't really get carried away. You're just kissing. The act of kissing is married to romance. Fling your arms around his neck and kiss his face. Hold her hand on the couch. Come up behind him and hug him, placing your chin on his shoulder and kiss his neck right in the middle of a crowd. The language of affection is telling the whole world, "He is mine and you can't have him!"

When you dated, did you kiss? Has it been something we neglected a bit after we were married? Sometimes it's a leap right to sex, because, that's all we have time for. Kids are napping, hurry. But between sex and not having sex there is a place called affection. It's something you do even when the kids are awake. Affection says, "Even after all this time, I'm still into you." It states, "I know we are watching a movie but I want to taste your lips for a second."

A great love story has a great beginning. Kissing keeps us remembering the beginning. Remember the first kiss? I took my girlfriend to a park, I had a boom box (it was the eighties), I played Chicago. We danced slowly. I went in for the kiss. We kissed for an entire song. I married her.

The next line of this Scripture is her dreaming about his love making. What we think about matters. She is stirring it up. She's also helping by telling her man that he rocks the bedroom. Of all the things we have to think about, here is one that is fun. Maybe push out the crowd of worries and anxieties and have a fling with your spouse right in the confines of your own mind. You see your thoughts about each other in this manner are speaking the forgotten language of passion. Our thoughts have the power to stir desire. So your sitting at a stop light on the way home from a crazy day, suddenly in your mind you're whisked away to *candles and white linen. He takes you suddenly... His body tangles with yours in...*HONK HONK, oops, green light.

Can we have a frank conversation about making love? I don't know who "frank" was or why his conversation was always a little more up front and honest, but I think we should imitate frank right now. There will be a few parts to this discussion.

Principle 11: Dare to fling open the flood gates of passion.

> Songs 8:6-7 (NET) [6]...For love is as strong as death, passion is as unrelenting as Sheol. Its flames burst forth, it is a blazing flame. [7] Surging waters cannot quench love; floodwaters cannot overflow it.

We Christians have the fire and the passion. Here our God compares our passion as unrelenting as the eternal fires of hell. The lusts on the big screen or on television will pale in comparison with the true godly passion that comes from the deep love that was imparted to you by God when you were born again. The world may have glimpses of passion, but the world's fires grow cold. They can't keep the spark. They will move from partner to partner trying to turn the counterfeit into something real. What the world calls passion isn't an eternal fire like yours is designed to be. Your fire could be flooded by a tsunami and it would blaze on all the more. The passion your marriage is capable of won't wane, but it will grow and grow through your whole life. The sexual desires are to be perfectly met by the spouse you chose, and God ordained this. He prepared them to be exactly the perfect sexual supplier you desire. Your marriage sex life can easily surpass the steamiest passage of that romance novel. There is nowhere else you will find a more fulfilling experience than with the spouse God chose for you. The next sexual encounter will be better than the last. Oh to know that God wills for your passion to be unrelenting.

In many ways religious teaching has placed a conservative, shameful, or even taboo filter on sex. But here we see God's true intention. He wants His children to experience the best of creation. Remember that God intricately created your sexual sensitivities, and the ability to experience that kind of pleasure.

> Song of Songs 8:4 (NIV) [4]Daughters of Jerusalem, I charge you: Do not arouse or awaken love until it so desires.

As we talk about passion, it's good to keep in mind that sometimes we are just not feeling it. Here the Scripture is telling us sometimes passion is sleeping. In other words, ladies, don't try and make it happen. Desire will well up in you and overwhelm you in its time. Ladies, when you *want* your man, it hits him in the deepest part of how God created him. What a man often wants most in love making is to be *wanted*. He can tell when you want him. But oh, how does love awaken? When will it awaken? Men are like, "Hey love, I'm awake, are you? Wake up!"

God has placed a path to awaken that desire in her. It is in her heart. She has God-given hungers that must be met. This is not about sex for her, but about being loved and pursued to benefit the relationship. A man's sexual drive is strong. It drives him. It will drive him to woo, pursue, romance and jump through many hoops for his bride. He loves her, and part of that expression is making love to her. Men and women are different for certain. A woman needs to have her desire stirred. A man's desire is mostly already stirred. His desire is in a non-stop blender.

A man's passion for his lover (wife of course) drives him into pursuit. The pursuit is designed to stir her passion, and awaken her love. This is the chase, it is healthy, and it should last your marriage a lifetime.

PURSUIT: The passion drives the man into pursuit.

One of the ways a woman's passion awakens is from the pursuit of her man. Sometimes a husband comes home all moody, kicks the dog, is snippy with the family, and then, when it's time for bed, he puts on his bedroom eyes for you, and in his best Joey from Friends voice he says, "How you doin'?"

Ladies, it's natural for you to think to yourself, "Wait, after how you've been treating me since you got home, and now you want to get into my knickers? Oh heck NO!" (Does anyone wear knickers? What is a knicker?)

The pursuit is the natural reaction to a man's desire. He isn't wooing and romancing you in a manipulating way, that is, just to get you in bed. Instead, it is the passion that has him thinking about you without ceasing which is designed to get him speaking in the language of passion.

> Song of Songs 8:4 (NIV) [4]Daughters of Jerusalem, I charge you: Do not arouse or awaken love until it so desires.

A woman's passion must sometimes be stirred, that is, awakened. Wives, it is totally normal that sometimes he is all fired up and ready, but you aren't feeling it. The Lord is saying to you, "Relax, don't awaken love until it desires." Husbands, don't take it personal when she isn't in the mood sometimes. She wears many hats, and there can be many stresses and

JASON AND KELLI ANDERSON

anxieties happening in her life. Sometimes the timing is just not right. Instead, listen to this Scripture, and let it inspire your desire to seduce her. This seduction takes place over time through both of you dipping into the language of passion.

Part of seeing that desire awaken is for the wife to be thinking in the language of passion. You can stir this. Keep in mind also, ladies, that your bodies are seasonal. Listen to your body. Women go through different seasons of sexual desire. If you are having a dry season, and by that I mean, you don't have the desire to have sex, I encourage you to investigate why. Ask the lord to show you why you have no desire. Maybe you are under a tremendous amount of stress, job, young kids, keeping the house in order, and at the end of the day, you are exhausted! The only thing you desire at the end of the day is, SLEEP! For you, you may have to schedule love making into your calendar. That may sound cold or insensitive, but, is it? If I have a plan, and I know that on Monday night, I am going to make love, then all day as I'm doing all my busy-ness, I'm thinking about him. Maybe have coffee in the later afternoon so that you have an extra boost of energy! Your husband and your marriage becomes first priority in doing this! Maybe, your lack of desire is related to hormone issues and older age. Go to your doctor, get blood work done and find out why you are dealing with this. Pray and ask God to help you. We don't get all the minerals, nutrients and vitamins we need in our world of processed foods and modified meats. Even if you do organic and non GMO it can help. Listen to your body; find a doctor that can help balance your hormones.

When a husband is pursuing and a woman is listening to her body, even stirring in herself, desire awakens. Desire will happen when it happens.

> Song of Songs 7:1-3 (NIV) [1] How beautiful your sandaled feet, O prince's daughter! Your graceful legs are like jewels, the work of an artist's hands. [2] Your navel is a rounded goblet that never lacks blended wine. Your waist is a mound of wheat encircled by lilies. [3] Your breasts are like two fawns, like twin fawns of a gazelle.

Solomon is speaking to her about her appearance. The language of passion is being spoken. Tell her she is pretty. We are all so insecure about our appearance. You are crazy about her. She needs to hear what you think. *Set my mind at ease; tell me you love how I look.*

The secret language of passion needs to be spoken. When we speak passion it stirs passion. Remember a time when passion was in abundance. When we think passion it stirs passion. There is absolutely nothing wrong with fantasizing about each other's love!

What is this language of passion? There was plenty of passion and fire when you were dating. Let's revisit the language of affection. You were affectionate to a fault. You thought about each other day and night. You spoke of each other's beauty often. These are speaking the forgotten language of affection. When you were dating you were on a forceful advance into each other's heart. He dropped off sappy notes on her car window. She spoke straight to his heart about the future. There were flowers and laughter and even, frolicking (whatever that is). She had his full attention. He was consumed in her eyes.

Do you remember your very first date, and you checked your outfit. "How does this look?" You asked someone else. You even ironed a shirt. Teeth were brushed. You washed the car. As a married man let us date our wives with the same attitude. Wash the car first. Wash you. Put on that cologne! Dress to impress.

It's normal in marriage to just throw on some sweats, haven't shaved in three days, and then we say, "Can we just stay home and binge a *net-flicker* show?" (I have to invent words to avoid copyright laws. I know it isn't called net-flicker.) That is *normal*, but you aren't after a *normal* marriage anymore. It's time to fill up your wife's pantry with all the goodness your love has to offer. Give her the dream. Give her a date so great she keeps taking pictures she can post online. She is screaming to the world, "Look, I am valued. I am loved."

Wives, dress up for your man. Do the primping you would do when you were just dating. Take his breath away. Remind him that you may be a mom, but you are still 100% woman. We can also communicate the language of passion in our appearance.

As years went by in my marriage I really let myself get pretty flabby. I'm not talking about you, I'm talking about me. We were busy. I was hungry. One day the Holy Spirit spoke to me about my health through a friend that was in town. "Bro, you need to take care of yourself if you are going to be preaching in the years to come." Hmmm. He was right. As it turns out, working out in the few minutes I have in a week, and eating healthy, well, it stirred some passion too. Our appearance is part of the language of passion. For me, it was about my health, but it rolled into some other benefits.

When we were dating we were showing our best face often. When you get all fixed up you are communicating the language of passion by saying, "Look at me. I want you to look at me. Say something about how I look. I value you greatly. I cared enough for you today to take a shower." Ha!

Remember when you were dating and you celebrated obscure anniversaries in your relationship. Like when you had bought her earrings to commemorate a three month and two day anniversary from the first day you held hands. You were nuts. Do it again. Buy her a bracelet in celebration that one month ago today you reset your marriage! You are still crazy for her, but you need to reconnect with that side again. Go pick up her favorite cup of coffee before she wakes up. Do you want to know what you are doing? Stirring. You are awakening love in each other.

On a great date a couple is having conversation that touches certain places in the heart and the mind. The famous first words of the date start with the bewitched daze of the man when he sees her. You can hear the song playing as she steps in high heels confidently into his view. He says something like "Oh wow, you're.. uh.. you're beautiful!" Passion worked in those days because it was being spoken.

You sit down for dinner. What does she like talking about? The kids? She has your complete attention and you are listening. You are hanging on every word. Ladies, you are laughing at his jokes. You are flirting with that man. You keep twirling your hair around a finger and batting your eyes. You put your hand on his arm and lean into him as you giggle.

Remember? This is the forgotten language of passion. We used to speak it, but it has just been awhile.

When the woman has been pursued passionately, loved to her soul, admired, accepted, looked at lovingly, spoken highly of, feels safe, and feels pretty, love awakens.

When the man feels... wait no, sorry, nothing to do here. He's awake.

We have talked about affection, passion and pursuit. Now let's talk about making love. When I was young we all saw Tom Cruise on the big screen making love in Top Gun. The girls at school talked about him, and the boys wanted to be him. On the silver screen he was an example of a great lover. We want to be great lovers. Not just great, we want to be the best. There is a problem though.

Many marriages are experiencing sexual frustration. It just hasn't been all it's cracked up to be. Oh well. So is life.

I'm asking you today to not accept mediocre. Or maybe it's good, but hey, it can always get even just a bit better. Let us, right now, set a goal to develop a great sex life. Your marriage sex life is going to be beyond your fantasy. You are going to crush Hollywood, and Tom Cruise is about to look like an absolute klutz at making love. Only the two of you can make this happen, and so let's talk about how.

Genesis 2:25 (NIV) [25]Adam and his wife were both naked, and they felt no shame.

First, let's get shame out of the bedroom. Say no to it. That naked shame, that vulnerable feeling, yeah, that's not normal with Jesus. He restored you to the "no shame" position. This is important for you two. Your spouse married you. It all started with attraction. Your spouse is attracted to you. It doesn't matter how you *think* you measure up to the beautiful people of the world, instead, you are beautiful to your spouse. Decide to let no insecurity creep into your bedroom. God created a magnetic attraction in which you were designed for each other, and the passion is God given. Your spouse is more attracted to how you look than anyone will ever be.

Imagine, God took time in His most powerful Word to tell us they were naked but had no shame. We all come in a package of insecurity about our bodies. We know God made us beautiful on the inside; we aren't always that sure about the outside. We need re-assurance. Speak the language of passion.

The language of passion doesn't just stir desire, but it sets its sites on fulfilling that desire. Don't forget, God invented the orgasm. This was His idea. We should, men and women, be magnificent at whatever we do. We are not playing second place to the Top Gun love scene. We are going light years past it. Be the best lover to your spouse. Be so crazy good he/she can't help but dream about it over and over.

Now listen, no pressure; you have lots of years to get this right, so we need practice. A great football team that wins the Super Bowl has to practice and try different plays. When I talk about different plays you cannot try things that violate the referee in your spouse, and coercion will probably backfire and be quite regrettable. You might say, "Can I try this?" She might be like, "What?? You're kidding right?" Uh-oh. The referee comes out on the field. That's a five yard penalty. In fact that penalty could haunt you for months. What matters is, what is comfortable for both. In Song of Songs it seems like there weren't many rules; there was all kinds of exploring and tasting. I think this is telling us that in marriage we can be confident that our restrictions are based on our personal preferences, and we learn to respect those restrictions with each other. What are you both comfortable doing? Play and practice. Communicate and take risks.

I was reading a marriage book written by a female author, and she talked about having been married for years and truly unhappy with her sex life. She was faking it. One day she just decided to tell her husband that she had been faking it. The response she received wasn't as scary as she thought it would be. Her husband was on board with learning and discovering how to get that engine revved up, if you know what I mean. If something isn't "working" for you, maybe speak up. Guide that man, he will do whatever you say, but he may need some direction. Men have no idea how a woman's body works, but I can assure you your husband is very, very, interested in learning all the intricate details of your desire. The football team just needs to try some different plays. Take the practice field, take your time, and explore.

Sometimes it is about endurance. Now if you want to learn how to run a marathon, you have to work your way up to it. If you only go jogging once every week, and only three weeks per month, you'll never get to that marathon level. We all laugh at the jokes about the man going to make love to his wife. He says, "I'll be back in two minutes." The reason that it is a universal joke is because it is universally true. Lionel Richie is going, "All night long...(all night..)" and the rest of us are wondering.. how? AC/DC says, "YOU! Shook me all night long."

You're like, "YOU! Shook me for a few minutes and then we watched the news till we fell asleep."

A man's endurance will greatly depend on his wife giving him the experience needed to learn to endure. Wind him up, and then let him come back down. Rinse and repeat. He can't help it you are so freaking hot. It's a compliment. Now take some time to figure out how you can get their together. Practice makes perfect.

Ladies, ego is a major part of a man's performance. He becomes better if he thinks that you think he's great. He will lose his mojo entirely if he can tell you are frustrated or just not into it. A man needs to hear that he is the best. He won't mind taking direction through encouragement. Ego desires to know there is no one or nothing else that compares to your man. He is the super hero of your life. When a man's wife loses herself in passion and the emotion of love making he will do much better. A man's ego runs deep and is like a spider web into many areas of his life. Do you think he's successful? Do you treat him as a strong man? Do you treat him with respect in front of others? Do you love and respect his parents/family? All of these things lean into his performance. When he feels like you see him as a man, he will be that man. Remember I said earlier that how we see someone determines what we can receive from them. It will greatly help you in the bedroom.

When I first married my wife I was quickly assigned the dishes. She was a better cook, so I cleaned up after. Early in marriage was this great big fight about how I put away the silverware wrong. In my household we took the dish washer basket that held all the silverware and we dumped the forks, spoons, knives and anything else that was in the basket into the drawer and closed it. Done. Apparently this wasn't right. My wife wanted each spoon to spoon the last spoon in the drawer, and by size. Placing the big spoons in the same section as the small spoons was of the devil. Dumping the silverware in the drawer was a stone-able offense. Same with forks. It is a very time consuming process to do this, but it is how she likes it. As she was yelling at me I was puzzled. *Look, I'll do the dishes however you tell me*, I just didn't know. Now I'm not just talking about dishes, am I? She may not want the silverware done *that* way. Her way may take more time, but if it pleases her, wouldn't you do it. Now it's a woman's prerogative to, at any point, switch the order around, change the pattern; what may have worked last time you did the dishes may not work exactly right this time. Just listen. Don't be so hell bent on saying, "Hey I know my way around the kitchen!" This is her kitchen. It's sacred... and it can be everything you ever wanted.

It is probably similar in terms of how you like the garage. The garage is my small domain in the house that I get to decide where things go. Get me? Maybe your next few sexual episodes aren't so much the sexual routine you've been used to. Maybe don't think of it as game day. Explore the strange unknown planet of your spouse's kitchen and/or garage.

Now I'm a pastor so the obvious view I have is you can't (don't ever) bring other PEOPLE into your sexual intimacy, and I think porn is exactly like bringing other people in to the bedroom. Our minds were not designed by God to process watching other people have sex, so it can make a mess of your brain. Intimacy is reserved for the two becoming one flesh. Two. You two.

Whatever else you decide to do in your bedroom is up to you and what you're BOTH comfortable with. If you want to bring in a hoover vacuum cleaner, well, I'm curious, but whatever. Go have fun.

See, this chapter wasn't so awkward.

Chapter Six

The Secret Language of "Us"

The day I agreed to marry Kevin was the day I accepted the fact that my life was not about me or what I wanted anymore. My 'big picture' had become about us and what we wanted, and through any situation, that is my focus.

Christy Messner - Married May 4, 1991

Disagreement. Disagreement is the root of a good fight. Sometimes we misunderstand. Sometimes we disagree. Sometimes that disagreement is an easy persuading away from agreement. Sometimes that disagreement goes deep. Disagreement is the result of difference. We are all different, so disagreement is going to happen.

In Scripture God show us there is power in agreement. Real power.

> Matthew 18:19 (NKJV) [18]"Again I say to you that if two of you agree on earth concerning anything that they ask, it will be done for them by My Father in heaven."

In this chapter I want to show you how that agreement is possible even though we are truly so different. Our individual worlds spoke different languages. We come into marriage with foreign communication. We must learn how to speak the same language. This will be the language of us. Imagine the potential. God puts this into play in our marriage as He asks us to leave our country, our people and our father's household. The problem with many marriages can be traced back to any one or more of these three. It's not that we are different. Of course we are. Instead, there are differences that we hold on to that should have been left long ago. The whole world talks about "compatibility." They ask, *are you compatible?* And so the world looks for like-minded people with shared interests, but we can all see from the data that the world's marriages are unhappy and failing. God offers a deep amazing secret here that we need to explore; a secret that may have been overlooked when you were married, but it is a retroactive revelation. In other words, as you understand this chapter you will be freed from the past, and the course in your marriage is going to be reset to God's design as though you had never missed a beat.

Before we were married it was the language of *me and mine.* In this chapter we will learn a new language, it is the language of *us and ours.*

I was speaking with a man about the deep rooted differences he and his wife were facing. He would say, "Well, her family would always.. But my family, we didn't think like that..." He was Italian; she was Mexican. "Italians don't really.... But in the Mexican culture, they will..." This is deep rooted disagreement, disagreement that can be traced to a family root or even to a culture, a people. They were each holding on to the language of me and mine. This causes confusion. God is certainly blending us all-together. In Christ He has made us all one family, one people. "There is no slave nor free, Greek nor Hebrew in Christ..." In Christ the two can truly become one.

Still, we are proud of our roots. We choose a point in time to say, "That's where my people came from." We might do DNA testing to find out where we came from. But really, that's a point in time. For instance, to say you're Irish is picking a point in time where some of your family used to live. But if you went back in history further, well, no one lived in Ireland. Keep going back, and if you're a Bible-believing fella, eventually you have to get to Noah. We can all DNA test right to that one guy, the boat builder. Further yet, we all go back to Adam and Eve.

Today, we pick a point in time to separate ourselves from other people. I'm this, but you are that. But really, we all go back to one, and we are all moving toward one. I'm technically a mutt. My genealogy is strongly headed back toward "one." I'm part this, some of that, some of this other. My wife is mostly Irish.

We grew up with different languages. Different traditions. Different philosophies. Family or no family, you grew up with a certain family identity. Any group will naturally grow an identity. Think about your high school football team. They had traditions, uniforms, logos, events, parties and the like. Their identity was different from the rival football team. Groups of people would root for their own team to win. We dress up to show the world which team we are on. We criticize the other team. We want the other team to get beat! This team mentality isn't much different when it comes to culture and family. The same basic principles apply here. Identity helps our natural God-given desire to be unique and magnificent.

When we get married we carry our old language into that new marriage, that new team. The differences are deep when they are attached to identity. Growing up, my wife didn't go to public school when she was in seventh grade. She went to a Christian school. As a kid she would have been privy to the conversations in her family of why that decision was made. She was programmed to believe that the private school was better for her future. So she wanted our kids to go to a Christian school until seventh grade, like she did. I wanted our kids to go to public school like me. My Dad used to say, "I want our kids to experience and grow strong in a real world setting." I had heard conversations about why public school was better. I was programmed. This was part of my childhood family identity. *Andersons go to public school.* As our oldest approached the age to start first grade, our tension grew. There were some arguments that really ran so deep, they were part of who we were as individuals. It's a simple example of difference that results in disagreement. Simple things, I know, but these are deep rooted disagreements. What about marriages where one is Catholic and the other Protestant? Both believe in Jesus and overlooked the differences while dating, but a person's faith is right at the root of who they are. Your husband wants to baptize the kids in the Catholic Church, and you're like, *wait what?*

In this way, every marriage is a blended family. Marriage takes two people and shoves their DNA, culture, background, and beliefs all in a blender and hits "CRUSH!" It feels that way. Today the phrase "blended family" is used to describe two existing family units coming together. You were married, had kids, and then that blew up. God brought you new love, and your new love has some kids too. And then the new kids have a father who isn't you. And your kids have a mother who isn't your new wife. And the new kids are living with some other kids. It is a blender. This can be far more difficult to make work than the first one which didn't work. You are going to *have to have* God's winning strategy here.

There are many different intensities of a "blended family," but God has a plan. God's solution is the same regardless of how distinctly different your traditions, backgrounds, or how many people are part of the merge. God drew the two of you together and He knows what you are capable of together. This is His plan. He will see you through. Things may seem impossible, but remember; in God's hands all things are possible.

In this chapter I want to talk about how the two begin to become one. There is a leaving so we can arrive where God wants us. Then we will take a look at how unconditional love becomes a key ingredient in our relationship with our extended family. This will bring great peace into your home.

> Genesis 2:24 (NKJV) [24]Therefore a man shall leave his father and mother and be joined to his wife, and they shall become one flesh.
>
> Genesis 12:1 (NIV) [1]The LORD had said to Abram, "Go from your country, your people and your father's household to the land I will show you.

God's very first marriage advice and then His conversation with Abram (later to be named Abraham) reveals God's pattern for your new family. Notice that in both cases here, there is a leaving of the old to create something new.

I want you to understand that the worlds philosophy is to blend the two different backgrounds together. I remember the very first time I was given an empty cup and told I could go get my own soda from the fountain drink bar. It was at a buffet restaurant called the Royal Fork. I was eight years old. It wasn't long until my brother and I were mixing all the sodas together into some hybrid Dr. Coke Dew Pepper Fresca. It was called a "Suicide." It really was a worse tasting soda, although we would pretend we liked it more. When you just mix up what is already existing it can be the same. Marriage suicide. Everything gets muddy. Everything is cloudy.

Meditate on redemption and God's family for a moment so that we can get the right godly picture. Jesus isn't making a suicide soda. He gives us a new cup. He says things like, "You can't put old wine into new wine skins." He says things like, "Old things have passed away (died) behold all things become brand new." Paul says in Galatians, "I was crucified with Christ nevertheless I live, yet not I but Christ that lives in me." In Christ there is a giving up and dying to who I once was as I step into the family of God. I am "being conformed into the likeness and image of the son." In Christ I must let go of my past. I take on a new identity. I have a new father. Now I'm not talking about marriage just yet. I'm talking about how God brings us into His family. He brings to me my actual identity as I learn to let go of who the world crafted me to be. He created me, and I trust Him to do the resetting. God is pushing out the past and revealing the new you. God's starting line isn't with *your* history and culture, instead it is *His* history and culture. His starting line is a clean slate, born of the Spirit.

Now let's see how this works in marriage. God is well aware of what this couple, Abraham and Sarah, are capable of. They will move into places of the Lord no one had gone. They will start something no one could start. They will be up against tremendous odds, but God saw that they would overcome with His help. God sees the same for you and your spouse. It's why you are up against such resistance. It is why things can seem so hard. Listen, Satan's kingdom is scared of what you two and your "blended family" will do to him. So Satan attacks, comes in like a flood, and he is trying to wear you down. But God has promised to "Bless you." He has promised to "Make your name great." "And you will be a blessing." Now here is your part. "I need you to move away from your country, your people, and your father's household."

Principle 12: Leave your old family identity behind.

This is not about a physical move for you. You don't have to leave your job, church, state, or whatever. If you love Michigan, by all means, stay. This is not a physical move, but it is a move. In order for you two to begin to speak this new language together, there is movement. Let's look at each one at a time: Country. People. Father's household.

First, He says to "move away from your country."

I maybe can trace my roots back 200 years. Even 2,000 years if I'm lucky. But God knew me before He created the worlds. In contrast, my body may have descended from this "race of people" or "culture," but I am born of the Spirit. As a believer, my country is the Kingdom of God. It has an even better heritage. A stronger legacy. "I am surrounded by a great cloud of witnesses." This means my family is massive and they are heroes of faith. You may be proud you descended from some hero in history. But those who believe in Jesus, according to Galatians chapter three, have descended from the great

Abraham. And he is the one who moved away from the old to embrace the new. In our family tree is the Messiah! That is a much deeper heritage and that is what God wants me to see. He says, "Leave your country..." If you bring it with you into your marriage, it becomes one more thing you are trying to blend in.

In the days before mass-communication, if a tribe was separated for a period of time the language between the two would begin to change. When we leave our country we depart from that language while our language now begins to go through changes. This has been shown to be true throughout history. The same is meant for your marriage. The movement will create an opportunity for a language to form that won't be from two separate backgrounds, but instead, will unite into one new language.

Your old country has a "way" of thinking, and a "way" of doing things. You may believe if you move away you are losing part of yourself. So this is how God works. Jesus says in Matthew 16 "If anyone wants to find himself he must first lose himself." When it comes to defining who you are becoming by these old roots you will never find who God has created you to be until you move away from your country. You see, for marriage to truly create something new out of the two separate people, God wants a fresh clean cup.

What I am saying is what God says. Still, Satan has created a real stronghold here to hold you back. In our society the message is quite opposite of what God has said is true. So this is our dilemma. This is why God says things like, "Be not conformed to the patterns of this world but be transformed by the renewing of your mind." Remember that the world's system for a happy marriage is broken. If the world's strategy is not working, then abandon it.

So you love your country of origin. You celebrate it. But you come to realize, your country doesn't define you anymore. You have left that country for God's Kingdom. You live in God's country now. People around us often try and hold us back. I grew up poor. Really poor. After being married for eighteen years a man came over to my house to bid a job who I had not seen since I was sixteen. When he saw where I lived, how I was dressed, he actually said to me, "Oh you've forgotten where you came from." *No, I am embracing where I came from. I am born of God.*

You are letting go of the old things as God creates something new. In this a marriage has a clean cup as God makes the two into one. Your new family identity cannot be found until the old is first *lost*. You need a gaping vacuum in your marriage identity! Your spouse didn't marry your whole country, she just married you.

Next, God says, "Leave your people."

Be each other's only friend for a while. This is God's natural way of causing the two of you to really press together. Sing along, "Just the two of us... we can make it if we try..." God needs some time and space to make the two into one. I know marriages that operate just fine where the two live very separate lives. They don't do things together. He has his life. She has hers. He has his friends. She has hers. But I don't want a *fine* marriage. I want an extraordinarily-passionate-best-friend-lover-unified-glorified-purpose-filled-Holy Spirit led- memorable-journey that the whole world envies. I want ONE! We desire God's perfect plan so we follow His patterns.

"They will be my people, and I will be their God." This is a running theme in the prophesy of the Messiah throughout the Old Testament. God couldn't wait to *call* you HIS PEOPLE. We all need a people, a sense of belonging. This is our friends and extended family. Think of it as the village of Abraham's life. Imagine Abraham and Sarah moving away from their country and their people. There was no social media to stay in touch. They wouldn't be watching the desert llama races with their friends on Thursday nights anymore. (Or whatever they did for fun.) Abraham and Sarah would have been in a situation where they were truly drawing together, leaning on each other, having no one else save God. "So what do you want to talk about?" Asks Abraham.

Sarah is rolling her eyes in a huff, "Abe, as I have asked about 50 million times, have you any idea where you are going?"

Abraham's hands went in the air, eyebrows jamming into his hairline bringing out those forehead lines she could map in her mind, "God said to go and *THEN* He would show me. So, YES.... but, well..." He paused and his tone dropped along with his eyes, and then with a big exhale, "no, I have no idea where we are going."

What does she want? Where is he going?

Leaving your people means creating relationship space for your spouse. Your best friend is now your spouse. Hmmm. We all have space in our heart for a super close BFF. So you have to clear out that space for your spouse. Maybe you were besties already, while dating. But if not, well, it's time to do some cleaning. This doesn't mean you send your old best friend a note, "I don't ever want to see you again." Truth be told, if you don't give your wife/husband first position, your spouse will probably begin to resent any time you spend with *that* friend or friends. Why? Because you have to become each other's number one! First place! Those super private conversations, heart pouring that you do with your best friend, yeah, that's a conversation for you and your spouse now. All that time you spend with your best friend, well, chop that way back. Your spouse gets those blocks of time now. You're best friend will say, "Ever since she got married she's changed. We don't really talk anymore." Good. That is what is supposed to happen. You'll reconnect with all of your friends. Relax. But right now we need some focus.

Sounds so simple doesn't it? Or maybe to some it just doesn't sound necessary. You and your spouse look at each other and say "Well, I don't agree with that. You have your friends, I have mine." But listen, God is trying to teach you the language of us. He is making ONE out of two. Us out of me. Our out of my. We out of I.

Part of this is recognizing that who you are around matters. There is an evaluation taking place all the time of who we let into our world. When you were single, who your friends were was up to you. You were the sole decision maker of who was in your world. But now that you are married, there is a natural sorting taking place. There is someone new voting on who will get to be in "our" world. So we kind of start from scratch as we take a moment to be each other's only friend. It's like the honeymoon; you unplug from life for a bit and are just with each other. It doesn't mean you hate your friends. You don't reject your friends. You love your people, but you are moving out. You love your parents, but you are moving out. You love your country, but you are moving out.

Think of it as a vacation from other relationships while God cements you together. Be each other's only. We can see some symptoms of the need to take time to do this as we look at newlyweds.

Your wife is angry. You can see it. She snaps, "I don't want you hanging out with him anymore."

What is that? What, you can't pick good friends?

"No, you just don't get him. It's just that he is, uhh, you know...listen, he's a great guy," you do your best persuading voice.

She puts her proverbial foot down, "You're not going out with him Friday. I don't trust him!" And that's that.

What is this? You know this is probably really not even about *that* friend. This is about the merge. Your friends are not her friends. When a spouse seems unreasonable in marriage, (making no sense at all) we have to look deeper. What your wife is saying is, "I NEED TO KNOW THAT I'M NUMBER ONE."

I know a man whose best friend his whole life was a girl. They grew up together. They went to the same school from first grade on. They were never romantic. The attraction just never happened. But they knew each other better than anyone. When he was married, or really, even engaged, the normal battle between his love and his friend began. It was heart wrenching for the new husband. It was heart breaking for his childhood friend. I mean, can't they still be friends? Is the new wife so insecure? Doesn't she trust them?

So the man went low key in it. He would find private moments to stay connected to his childhood friend. He was hiding this relationship from his wife. It was innocent, but deceptive. They would meet up. It was like a friendship affair. Nothing romantic was going on with his childhood friend, and yet, it was breaking everything in the new marriage apart.

There was a place in his heart he would not give to his wife. One day he was discovered, seen hanging out with the old friend.

"Oh, we just happened to run into each other," he lied. But somehow, the wife knew he was lying. They always know. She was ready to divorce him, not because he cheated, but because he betrayed her trust. What's the big deal? Well, it is the merge, and it needs to be embraced.

The problem wasn't that she didn't trust him. In the world's view, the new wife has been unreasonable. *Why can't he still have his old friends?* That space in his heart now belongs to his wife. That real-estate was purchased with a lifelong commitment when he said *I do.* Marriage requires all of you; the whole heart. She gets first place. The first year of marriage will seem like a bit of friendship vacation. Like the new couple is pulling away from other relationships. This is the natural progression. We've all seen and wondered about it when couples do this. Newlyweds have been criticized for it. But really, something new is being established. The people must be left. When the husband finally gave up this position, he was free to give that space to his wife, and the result was success. They were able to move their relationship to the place God had called it, that is, higher.

Furthermore, who you are around influences you greatly. You are headed into a new season, and there will need to be the right people established by God to help you. Divine relationships. When Jesus switched seasons from being a carpenter and into His ministry, He went and found new friends. As you are married, a natural transition of friendship begins. Just like when you moved from grade to grade in school. Each new season there is a re-sorting of our relationships. Marriage is a brand new season. There will be a season where your spouse is your only friend, and then after the friendship vacation, new relationships will begin to emerge. I recommend following Scripture of course, and making sure your new people are God's people. God has a people for you! Jesus didn't let just anyone be one of his twelve disciples. He stayed up all night praying, and then chose His twelve. Great destiny means surrounding ourselves with the right relationships. Leaving your people creates relationship space for God to bring in His people for you.

Leave your people.

Next we "Leave your father's household." In other words, we leave mommy and daddy and cleave to each other. I'm not sure really what cleave means. I don't think it has any root or relation to the word cleaver, although a cleaver may be necessary to cut the umbilical cord.

> Ephesians 2:19 (NKJV) [19]Now, therefore, you are no longer strangers and foreigners, but fellow citizens with the saints and members of the household of God,

God told Abraham to "Leave your father's household." God wants to be your household now. You always honor your parents. You love them. It is a commandment of God. You care for them as they get older. When Jesus was on the cross, He took care of some last minute housekeeping as He was redeeming the entire world. He gave His mom to be cared for by His disciple John. "John, this is your mother now. Mother, here is your son." And care for her John did.

In a marriage the two are leaving mommy and daddy and joining to each other. The Bible teaches us in Ecclesiastes a "cord of three strands is not easily broken." In other words, it is husband, wife and Jesus. Take some time and weave that together. There is no room for mommy or daddy in the new rope. For some, mom and dad have been the center of their whole existence until now. For others, a parent or both were entirely missing. Whatever the case, it is in the separating that the joining can begin. When one spouse drags a parent deep into the marriage the joining suffers. The wife needs to be the woman in your life now. It can't be mom. The husband must be the man in your life now, it cannot be dad.

Your mom and dad may have a hard time giving up this slot. It is painful for them, and it will be painful for you one day when your children are married. Mom and Dad may try and weave themselves back in. This is normal. Don't be mad at them. Love them. But the leaving must still happen.

When my son went to college I was all broken. I wanted him to stay. But I needed him to go. In the same way your parents may want you to stay, but they *need* you to go. You will have to do what is BEST for everyone, and not trying do what everyone is wanting. What is best is, mom and dad, I have to go now.

This means a massive priority shift. Husbands, your wife is far and above number one. Wives, your husband is numero uno. Jesus first, obviously. My point is, God knows we have to cut the umbilical cord so that we can really draw together. In some marriages we see what is called enmeshment. Mom and dad or extended family is just far to woven into the fabric of the marriage.

I remember a night where my wife was in labor with our first child. We arrived at the Desert Samaritan Hospital at 10pm on

March 11, 1997. Labor was slow. There were long stretches in the night where my wife and I wandered the halls of the hospital. Me, I was squeaking along the wheels of the I.V. that was carefully attached by a long dangling transparent tube to her wrist. Her, she was stopping to lean against a cold window, another contraction shortening her breath. Moms and dads had all gone home to bed. There was no one we could call on the phone. Everyone we knew was fast asleep. Nurses were busy about the rooms. The halls were dark. My wife in pain. Me helpless, only offering my concerned look and deep sighs. We only had each other that night. And God. There was no one else we could lean on. For eight hours we were isolated. Us and God. Tired. Nervous. We had each other. Up until that night, when there was turmoil or trial I could call my dad. She could call her mom. Not this night. We were just kids. Foolish. We had no answers. We had no experience to lean on. We had each other and God. And something magical happened. A new language began to take shape that no one knew but us. It would be our language. She learned to look and lean on me in tough times. I was the new man in her life. I was the one who would be by her side through anything. She was the new woman in my life. She was *my everything*. She was giving her very best for our future child; literally laying her life down for our family. *Our* new family. Something brand new. Magic.

Leaving your country, your people, your father's household; this is also going to be a renewing of your old thinking. We carry from our old roots things like our faith, our traditions, and our philosophies. We have learned how to love from these patterns. We may or may not have had a family that forgave. Maybe in your household growing up there were fights but no one ever said, *I'm sorry.* Maybe in your country you are all hot-headed and emotionally-driven. We all are born into and come from generations of established patterns and philosophies that needle their way through our thinking and actions. But God has different ways of thinking, and His thoughts and philosophies work better. So He gets us to re-identify. He relabels us as His children. This way, no matter the background of any individual, God can have a fresh start and help build a legacy into each and every marriage by transforming us out of the old and into the new. It is a rejection of the philosophies that were programmed into me as part of my identity so that God can re-identify me with how He created me.

A couple I know married. She was a career woman, college graduate, ambitious. He came from a home where his mother didn't work, and his father did. The wife was raised by a single mom. When this newlywed couple was married she found herself pregnant. She planned her six weeks maternal leave, and then she was back to work. Her new husband had a meltdown. "You're going back to work?"

Two different households had two different philosophies. In the world's system we would sit down and sort it out to a reasonable conclusion. In God's system of marriage, we abandon ourselves to find out what God wants. This one difference in upbringing became a divorce-able difference. Her working or not working was a deal breaker. This was one of many family and culture defining differences that came into the merge that were being blended into oblivion. They were trying to marry two countries, two peoples, and two households. In the rising temperature they came in for marriage coaching. How can these two possibly become one? If both are willing to die to what they already knew they could place it in God's hands. God is taking them to a land that He will show them. The Spirit has desires inside of us. Relax and listen to the Spirit's desire for your family. God isn't *recreating* your house and upbringing. He is creating something new, something that will play right into His destiny for you.

We just need the two to become one. For this reason a man (think of this as mankind, it applies to both) will leave father and mother and cling to each other. The clinging happens as a result of the leaving. The movement draws us together. Both of us are committing to God's best for us.

In God's house there is supply, love, forgiveness, hope, thankfulness, mercy, grace, prosperity, peace and patience. The attributes and patterns of God's household invade our home because we walked into them. This is the land we moved into. This is who we are now.

"Get out of your country, leave your people, move away from your father's household."

The moving gets us to "us" faster. We. Our. Our money. We already know about your family and my family. We are becoming "our" family. Our dreams. Our destiny. Our friends. Our traditions. Our philosophy. Our faith.

This is a concept, not a law. It is a goal that will be attained over time. Abraham and Sarah left, but after five minutes you could still see the old. It was right there. Be patient. After a day of walking they really aren't that far away. *Walk* through this. It is a journey. The journey begins with the decision to make God's country your country, God's people your people, God's Household your household.

The goal is "our" everything. "Our" happens faster as we move away from your country, your people, and your father's house. It's not "my country." It's ours. Our people. Our father. Our Jesus. Our promises. Our marriage. Our life. Our children... Our Christmas. Our vacation. Our house. Our family. Our.

Reinvention: The power of letting go of who I used to be is reinvention. The two of you now have the opportunity to allow God to reinvent you. He is taking these two different jars of clay and forming them into one jar of clay. You had a family identity. But now you leave all of that and cling to one another, and you have the opportunity to create a new family identity. Your whole life you will go through many changes. In and out of season our desires move around. Through the years we grow. I used to hate salmon. Now I like it. Our preferences change. Reinvention allows us to become who God is growing us into. If we remain where we were we become stuck. Abraham and Sarah were moving. Their life had been recalibrated to an upward trajectory. In the same way, God has reinvented you, made something brand new, unique, He brought you together. If you allow Him, He is going to move you and position you for the dreams and desires He brought you together for.

Abraham and Sarah were "uprooting," as they left. In order for these two separate trees to move closer to each other, they must be uprooted. Uprooting sounds painful, unstable, and insecure. Still, it is in the insecurity that we quickly lean into one another. It is in our moments of instability that we rely upon each other. It is in our uprooting that we can be replanted together, having our roots mingling below the surface of the soil. Will you allow the Lord to do this in your marriage? When you are uprooted from the old ways of thinking God can begin to nourish you with new thoughts. Not everything you are letting go of is going to be removed, but are you willing to let him remove those things that are not part of your future?

"Well that's not how I did it! In my family we were taught that..." Uh oh. Recognize the word "my" in that sentence? You have a new family now. God wants access to do new things in this new marriage and family. He is a God of doing new, creating new, empowering and enriching newness. If you have a spirit of heaviness, He gives you a garment of praise. He clothes us differently. What worked yesterday may not necessarily work tomorrow.

Principle 13: Dare to speak a different language about each other's parents.

The brilliance of God sending us moving away from our father's household is the healing that happens in the heart. What I mean is, there are no perfect earthly fathers. Jesus referred to earthly fathers as "evil." You married someone who had a dad they may have never met, was never there, hated them, beat them, or were absent emotionally. Or maybe their dad was the greatest dad ever. Still, there are many things that have gone wrong in most people's childhood. These hurts and inadequacies haunt your future; including your marriage. As adults we still operate from the insecurities and pains left by the gaping love holes in our hearts.

My dad's mom left when he was three. She promised she would come back the next Saturday. My dad waited outside of their one bedroom house in rural Norther Wisconsin, staring down a lonely two lane crumbling road every Saturday for over a year. His father couldn't pull him away. "She's coming, I just know it." She never came.

When my dad was married, he pushed my mom away. Each year that they grew closer together he would push her out of his heart. He didn't know why. One day the Holy Spirit revealed to him why he was having a hard time letting her in his heart. He loved my mom deeply. Why wouldn't he let her in? Suddenly the answer came to him. *The women in your life will leave you.* That was the deep philosophy of his heart. Keeping her out would be a self-fulfilling prophesy. By pushing her away she would eventually leave. He had pushed his own mom out of his heart because the pain was unbearable. God was restoring my father. He had to move away from what he had learned and take on God's philosophy. God, a God who never leaves or forsakes. It is a reprogramming in our heart. We can see that he *had* to leave his father's household and let Father God redefine him. He had to walk away from what he knew so He could take on what God knows. The healing stimulated him to track down his mom. He found her. He had forgiven her. He loved her unconditionally. He was able to spend some time with her in her final years.

This includes loving the in-laws unconditionally!

What is it about married couples and the in-laws? This can be a lot of tension in a marriage. It's the big joke; the wife can't stand her mother-in-law. The mom and the wife are competing for the first position in the husband's life. The same can be true of a daughter and her father. This in-law tension can cause lots of fights. Or maybe it isn't all that deep. Maybe you just can't seem to get along with your in-laws. Maybe it has something to do with how mean they have been, or they rejected you, you just weren't good enough for their little Jimmy. Or maybe they were bad to your spouse. Whatever it is, there can be a lot of drama surrounding the in-law thing. Can we solve this once and for all please? Yes. With just a few mental adjustments of rejecting the world's philosophy and taking on God's solution, you can be free of this fight once and for all.

Parents aren't perfect. As we take on God's country, people, and household, we find ourselves free of the pains and rejections of the past, healed. But, because each of you is a product of the family setting you were raised in, there is a temptation to carry one another's offense about each other's family. Your spouse might be over it, but you're still mad. For instance, a husband is mad at his wife's father because he wasn't there for her. She's over it. It is often harder to forgive someone for hurting another person than for them hurting you. The husband is being a protector. It is the wrong move though. Love must invade every area of your family. Let me explain more.

You walk in and your wife has that exasperated look, "Ugh my mom just makes me so mad! She reminded me again today that I married the wrong man. I'm like, 'Mom, I love him, this was my choice, you need to get on board.'..."

So now you are rejected and mad at her mom. *She hated you from the beginning!* The principle I want to share with you is *loving parents unconditionally.* They may be great. They may be a mess. They may be worthy or unworthy of your love. Love them anyways! Anything outside of loving them unconditionally will become a thorn in your marriage. The Bible teaches, "Honor your father and mother that it might go well with you." We want it to go well, right? This is going to be expressed through how you speak. Remember, we are daring to speak a new language! How do you speak to your in-laws, and how do you speak to your spouse about your in-laws? We know the world's language for this. I'm inviting you to *speak a different language, a secret language* that will bring healing and wholeness to your marriage. Essentially, there is a path to peace here that we pursue.

Now if a man thinks badly of his wife's parents, and says it, he is essentially rejecting his wife since that is where she came from. Whatever is wrong with them is attached to her. The rejection of your spouse's parents is an unseen force at work against your spouse. A woman deep down thinks that if you don't like her parents then you don't like her. It is the same for a man. It is a sub-conscience conclusion, meaning, they don't actually know that they feel that way.

The right solution for this man is to defend *her* parents. "You know your mom is so smart. She just wants what's best for you. I mean, hey, no question about it, I married up. Don't let it get to you." He smiles and puts his hand on your hand, "I'll win her over eventually. We just keep loving them, love always wins. Just let it go, baby."

You just drew your wife closer to you because you loved her mom without condition. Her mom doesn't even like you. Well done. It is easy to dislike the people who don't like us, but Jesus showed us a different way. Take no other view with your spouse's parents.

Maybe your husband's dad is being a complete jerk. Suddenly the wife is so ticked. "I don't want him over at our house next weekend. He's a jerk to you." Hmmm, maybe the husband shouldn't tell her about all the drama with his dad. The husband is over it, but she is still mad. There is a better response for her. It would be better if she found good things to say about his dad. "Baby, your dad is an incredible man.

Maybe he isn't perfect, but you know he just wants to bring out the best in you, to push you. It is probably all he knows from how he was raised. Let's just put on our smiles and keep loving him." The husband is connected to his dad. Same DNA. There is a hidden part of us that wants our spouse to love where we came from.

The goal is simple. Love your spouse's family unconditionally; brothers, sisters, cousins, parents, all of them. Speak highly of them.

If the wife's parents need a good talking to because of how they keep sugaring up the kids until they look like balloons, then let the wife do it. Each should fight with their family. If the husband's brother is being a pain, the husband should handle it. The wife stays out, and loves unconditionally. She must refuse to pick up the offense. If she gets all upset then her husband will take a defensive posture and has positioned himself against his spouse. This is dysfunctional. Instead, the husband is in a battle with his own brother, and she is working to calm him down.

In a Blended Family, Express Lovingkindness to Their Children!

For blended families the same is true for your children. Many times the new husband steps right into a disciplinary role with his new wife's kids. She's been complaining since they started dating about how her son won't do what she says. He comes in to fix the problem with some old fashioned discipline. They got married, the ring is on, and the gloves come off.

"I'll teach that boy a thing or two," He is rolling up his sleeves.

He thinks he is helping, but really he puts his wife into a mother bear posture. *She was a mom before she was your wife.* Back off bro. She has to protect her son. Remember, her son has been here longer than you have, and she is built to protect him and give up her life for him. Suddenly the husband, who is supposed to be a protector, has become the adversary. It would be better for you to let her discipline her children, and you be the loving full of grace guy. She may even ask you to get involved.

She says, "He's such a little brat." It would be so easy for the new husband to jump in and say *I agree, that little kid gets under my skin. And you know what his teacher said to me.* Uh oh. Trap! Red alert! You are talking about her son!

Let me suggest another response. He replies, "That kid is brilliant. I love being around him. He's such a ham. You know this transition may be hard on him, but love will win. He's just a strong leader."

One of the greatest ways you can love someone is to love their children. Express that love through kindness. Remember it is the Lord's *lovingkindness* that draws us near. In this you will be drawing your wife and her children to you like a tractor beam.

Now that we have left the old, let's take a look at what the new looks like. I want to show you the brochure of where we are going. It is a land flowing with milk and honey. You ready? Great, here we go.

Chapter Seven

The Secret Language of Marriage Expectations

"When it comes to my husband, I'm so glad God gave me what I needed and not what I thought I wanted!"
Pastor Tammy Zubeck - Married since March 4, 1995

Marriage should be full of joy and happiness. Sure there is resistance, I mean, embraced resistance makes us all stronger and propels us to new heights. We don't avoid resistance, we overcome it. In this chapter I want us to be reprogrammed in our expectations about marriage. I want us to realize there is a blissful happy fulfilling marriage just under the surface, waiting to be discovered. Next, I want you to know you already have everything you need. It is just a matter of learning how to uncover that experience.

Survival. This is the problem of accepting a mediocre average marriage. How are you doing? "We are surviving..." If you listen to how people talk about marriage, you might believe the whole world of married couples seem to be just barely making it. Enduring. Persevering. "We didn't give up," they say. *Just hold on and you'll make it.* When you feel like you can't take anymore, just shove a little more down inside.

"Man, marriage can be hard," leans in your uncle, he stares down as he wrings his hands, his tone even and serious.

You go to a marriage conference and the first line is, "Listen, marriage is work! Don't think for a second it is going to be easy." *Wait what? People don't like work. We like play. We like fun. We like rest. I went to work, I don't want to come home to more work.*

You are in pre-marital counseling. The counselor says, "The first three years are the hardest. For some it can be the years of torment." Hmmm. *Gee, thanks for that.*

Your grandparents sit you down, "Being married isn't rainbows and butterflies. There will be days when you just want to walk away. You will want to throw open the car door and start running down the street screaming. But don't. Stay." *Uhhh, really?*

The wife is described as the "ball and chain," or "the boss", or "my old lady." The husband is Homer Simpson. This isn't a good sales pitch at all. I mean, married couples are always trying to fix up the single people so they can get married. Why? *So you can join us in our pool of pain!*

Remember the dreams of a child? *Happily ever after*. That is the dream. *I just want to be happy.*

Marriage is designed by God to be all that you dreamed when you were young. The world's message is to lower the bar so that all you expect is a prison with a life sentence.

Marriage is the happiest most fulfilling decision of my life, save my decision for Jesus Christ and the Andy's Custard that opened up down the street. MMMMM, custard. (My best Homer Simpson voice.) God has a marriage for you that is going to escape the mundane. Marriage isn't going to be work. It's going to be rest. It's the place you go for recharge. Your marriage in God's hands is peace, joy, happiness, and destiny. God's desire for your life is that you have the very best; that you are living in His inheritance, in His promised land. Do you hear it? This is the new language, how we speak about what we expect from marriage. The world is saying to expect drama and trauma. But not us. We are learning a new language. We are going to start to see what we say!

Principle 14: Speak the Language of Your Marriage Expectations.

Don't say what you have about marriage. Don't say what the world expects your marriage to be. Say what you want your marriage to become. Speak out loud. Say what God says!

When Abraham and Sarah left their country, their people, and their father's household, they went to the Promised Land. This is where you are going! God's best for you. Your spouse is the person God has chosen to be with you to enjoy the land of fulfillment. Your spouse was the missing piece in your destiny.

We can choose to accept God's desire for our life, or we can choose to do our own thing. We can expect that marriage is going to be incredible, or we can expect it to be tough. We will have what we expect. We can believe all of the things the world says about marriage, or we can believe what God says. When we believe what God says, then we will recognize that adversity in our marriage isn't coming from God, but from the world, wrong beliefs, and the enemy trying to bring division. When we know this, we will stand strong in God's promise for He IS FAITHFUL.

> Ephesians 6:12 (NIV) [12]For our struggle is not against flesh and blood, but against the rulers, against the authorities, against the powers of this dark world and against the spiritual forces of evil in the heavenly realms.

Your struggle isn't with your spouse. It really isn't. There is something deeper at work here. You aren't fighting with people, but with the enemy. If you want to win you have to know where the real fight is. The enemy gets us thinking wrong and feeling wrong. If you are eating from the bread of wrong thinking and feeling, well, before you know it you're fighting with your spouse. The real fight is not with your wife. The real fight is against the divider. Your real battle is with your ability to remember the right stuff and forget the wrong. The battle is with forgiveness, hope, kindness, and love. Christ in you is defeating the wrong beliefs and patterns. You don't fight with your spouse; instead your spouse has the arms you run to. Now you will still fight, but take a moment to look at what you are actually fighting. You are fighting some wrong belief in you, or some wrong thinking in them, or probably some of both. Or maybe you're just not talking. (See chapter one) Hmmm, let's look at this then.

Psalms 112:3 (NASB) [3] Wealth and riches are in his house.

So where are the wealth and riches? Right under your nose. The wealth you seek is already in the gift that God has given you; your spouse and children. We are programmed to look outside of what we have to find happiness. It is the *grass is always greener on the other side* mentality. And so people search for happiness not realizing where true wealth has been hidden. A man pursues his ambitions leaving his house far behind. The children don't know their dad. The wife doesn't see her husband. He gains great worldly wealth, but isn't truly happy. His wife has divorced him. She says, "You give the best of you to your work, and the rest of you to your family, and I'm tired of getting the leftovers." This man at the end of his life finds great regret in his success.

Principle 15: Discover the riches in your spouse.

A marriage has fallen into a famine, and the wife has found herself feasting on the interested eyes of another man. She is starving to be looked at again. She is hungry to be heard. It seemed so innocent until he stole that kiss. *It felt so real! Doesn't God want me to be loved?*

Stop, what does the Word say? "Wealth and riches are in your house." The happiness you seek can be found in your spouse. It really is in there. God placed wealth and riches right in your home.

God said, "I will bless you in the land I have given you." He already gave it to you, and it is in that land that the blessing flows. All of what you are searching for is already there; you just haven't seen it all. It's not in some other land. The wealth and riches are right inside your house. Where? That's just it, it is time to go hunting. God has given you everything you need for life and godliness. He has blessed you with every spiritual blessing in the heavenlies.

In 2014 a couple in California discovered an old box buried right in their own backyard. They had lived there for many years and never noticed it before. They had a decent-sized piece of land and much of it was left in its natural state. But on this one particular day they noticed just a corner of some box peeking out of the ground. They dug it up. It was heavy. Really heavy for its size. Heaving it out of its dirt mold they pried it open to discover it was filled with weathered gold coins. Astonished they continued to dig around to find many more of these boxes buried just below the surface. In all they had found 11 million dollars in gold.

Before this they were not living in luxury. They lived an average somewhat meager life of work and play. I imagine they were probably, like the rest of us, going to work for the pay check. There were probably days they didn't have enough and so they would look for others ways to earn some money. Who knows, maybe they would buy lottery tickets hoping their number would come up and they could escape the rat race of living check to check. All along they were millionaires already.

God is saying the same thing to you. The wealth you are looking for, the riches, they are already yours. You are a millionaire. You have already been made joint heirs with Christ. You need look nowhere but right inside that land God has given you. What do I mean? Instead of trying to find happiness and fulfillment somewhere else, it can be found right here in your marriage. Right here in your family. The greatest joy a person will truly experience is literally right under your nose. Not just love, not just acceptance, value, hope, peace, and rest, but also the fruit, the blessing, the prosperity, the dollars, everything can be found in what God has already given into your hands. Remember He has blessed the works your hands. He said to Abraham, "I will increase you exceedingly." This promise is on you and your spouse.

How do I find it? Well, if I told you there was 11 million dollars buried somewhere in your back yard, how would you find it? You would search relentlessly. You would discover it. Then you would uncover it. Then you would redeem it. Paul expresses it more clearly for us when he said, "We have this treasure in jars of clay." The treasure you seek, the wealth and riches, they are just inside of you and your spouse. Your spouse partnered with God is absolutely capable of seeing every God given desire and dream of your heart be fulfilled. She is exactly the gift God brought you and she is filled up to overflowing with the wealth and riches you desire.

The man of your dreams that you married, that same man is capable of anything. That wife of yours contains limitless possibilities. Your spouse is filled with treasure. The wealth and riches are right there, inside of them, waiting to be sought out. The man you married has genius in him, the blessing of Abraham on him. The anointing to be both Priest and King has been given to him. These things need only be discovered and uncovered by you. That woman you married, multiplication and increase is part of her destiny. Her abilities surpass your wildest imagination because of Christ in her. But you must search for those abilities. You have to dig around. Think about what God has said about your spouse. That they are *more than an overcomer*. They can *do all things through*

Christ who gives them strength.

The treasure really is in a jar of clay. It's a mud pot. The mud pot forgets things. The mud pot makes big mistakes and puts his not-so-treasured foot deep into his muddy mouth. But inside, there is treasure. We have grace for the clay, while we dig in the dirt to find the value. If we always just look at the clay we will find our marriage quite literally stuck in the mud. Your wife is capable of the impossible. Your husband can do anything. Anything.

We say, "Well I'm not sure my husband can really do that." *Why? The same Spirit that raised Christ from the dead dwells in them!*

I started talking in chapter one about the need for us to dig in to find each other's desires. Now let us take it a step deeper. We are digging into our spouse to reveal the deep well of riches that God has placed in them. God said it. We should believe it.

Your faith and words can draw the treasure to the surface of your spouse. Don't say what your mom says about your spouse. (I mean, if your mom doesn't like him.) Don't come into agreement with negative things about your spouse. Instead, say what God says, and believe what God believes. He says your spouse is more than an overcomer. That God's favor is on them. Jesus said, "Greater things will your spouse do than I have done." I'm paraphrasing. Your spouse will believe your words more than any other words including their own thoughts. If they think they are a loser, your words can refute and defeat that. Your husband is not Homer Simpson. He is not dumb. He may think he is, though. Your job then is to get him to believe that He has the mind of Christ.

I spoke to a woman who had failed her medical certification exam. She said "I know the material, but I'm terrible at taking tests." That is the mud talking. The treasure inside is not terrible at taking tests. So I challenged the label. I said, "Change how you label yourself. You are great at taking tests. Jesus is in you. His mind is your mind. He knows all things." She dug deep and later would pass the test. All that happened was she began to expect something different. Your spouse may need a new label, and you are the perfect person for the job. You can retitle him. All of us believe what others believe about us. It is natural. Unfortunately, most of the world's voices don't believe what God says about us. So when you come into agreement with what God says about your spouse, you release supernatural power.

You can believe your spouse's treasure right into redeeming it. When I say redeem it, I mean that what is in them comes into play and begins to produce value. A woman who believes she is unintelligent won't try for that promotion, or pursue that idea for a business, because she doesn't want to fail. A person who is full of courage will try. When the treasured courage is revealed because ability has been discovered and uncovered, then the person will redeem that ability. They will take action and start that idea or pursue that promotion. Faith cannot be derailed by failure. A person who believes in what God has placed in them can take risks without the fear of failing. Failing isn't bad; it's just part of trying. Courage keeps trying despite failure. Faith perseveres and is not derailed by failure; it just tries again. Lots of our heroes in the Bible had failure. Even Jesus went to cities, preached, healed, and the city rejected him. He didn't fail. He was still going! Faith keeps going because it has no choice but to redeem the qualities and abilities that have been given. It puts those abilities into action.

The reason a person won't press into a trajectory of elevation is not the fear of failure but the fear of confirmation. They already believe that they are a failure, so they won't try things because they don't want to actually confirm what they "know" about themselves. What they know about themselves isn't actually true, since God speaks truth! Take a single man who won't approach a girl he is attracted to. He isn't truly afraid she will reject him. That part is just kind of on the surface. Rejection can't be the root of the fear because, logically speaking, he doesn't want to be with a girl that doesn't like him anyways. Approaching her is just part of sorting out the girls who don't like him back. Who cares if she doesn't like him? In fact it is a benefit to know that she isn't interested, now he can move on. So what is the root fear? What keeps a single man from approaching a girl he is attracted to? The real reason a man doesn't approach the girl is because he believes he's worthless. His fear is that she will confirm that belief. It is the fear of confirmation. Well, now that he's married to you, you can undo those wrong beliefs and get those God given abilities into motion. The reason people don't try new things isn't the fear of failing, but instead, it is the fear of confirming the belief that they are a failure. Do you see the difference?

So here's my point. When you speak this new language into your spouse they will begin to believe things about themselves. In that faith comes the discovering and uncovering of the greatness that is in them. As they have faith in that greatness, redemption of those qualities becomes necessary. In effect, they are no longer afraid to act, but instead they are compelled to act on the ability that has been revealed. That ability is the power that Paul talked about in Ephesians when he said:

Ephesians 1:18-20 (NIV) [18] I pray that the eyes of your heart may be enlightened in order that you may know the hope to which he has called you, the riches of his glorious inheritance in his holy people, [19] and his incomparably great power for us who believe. That power is the same as the mighty strength [20] he exerted when he raised Christ from the dead and seated him at his right hand in the heavenly realms...

Focus in on the *power* here for a second. Paul is praying that you might "know the great power for us who believe." It's the same power that raised Christ from the dead. That power is in your spouse. They just don't know it. And maybe you didn't know it. But for a believer, it is in there. Your husband has authority over your body. Your husband can pray for you and see miracles. The power is in them. Why don't we see it more? Well, it is because we don't actually believe it. We don't yet "KNOW" what Paul was praying we would know.

Paul was helping them see what was in them. The power they already had was something they didn't yet KNOW. Your spouse just doesn't KNOW what they are capable of. You have a genius of immeasurable infinite ability on the inside sleeping right next to you. Paul recognized he had the shovel to help these people discover what was in them already. You also need to take up your shovel! What I mean is, start digging in your spouse to reveal what is in them through your faith in them. Believe in the unseen! Say it out loud, prophesy into their future by saying what Jesus says about them. "Greater things can you do, baby, than even Jesus did!"

As the treasure is revealed, know that the treasure in your spouse is for you, and the treasure in you is for her. The land is flowing with milk and honey. When you truly believe in your spouse, and you are voicing it, and they are beginning to believe it, there will be a flow from your house of milk and honey. Now without going through the doctrinal theological Hebraic meaning of this phrase "milk and honey," I'd rather suffice it to say, it is the pleasure of the land. It is the sweet stuff. You will feed on the abundant goodness of the land if you can get the lid off the pot of your spouse and let what is inside them come out. You don't do this through criticism, but instead, through faith. Belief. Your wife will become the cream in your coffee. Your husband is the ranch dressing to your french-fries. God has planned this all along. He has hidden sweets inside your spouse that you didn't even know you needed or wanted. He has hidden gifts in your wife that will be unlocked in some future season of marriage that will bring you a sense of fulfillment and joy you never knew you would even desire. Your spouse is the "mother load" of bewildering and startling jewels and gold. "Well something just feels like it's missing in my marriage." Sure, that just means you need to dig deeper. It's in there!

As desire in you stirs for new things, and through the years, just look at your spouse and know that God has already hidden just what you needed right inside of them. Discover it. Uncover it. Redeem it. Milk and Honey.

God has a land of riches for you, in your spouse, in your children, in your house, and in HIS HOUSE for you, the great storehouse for your family.

Chapter Eight

Understanding Him

"We were the best of friends before we became romantically involved. All of these years later, we're still the best of friends and still very much in love. We feel being great friends first gives the marriage a very strong footing."
Ken and Leslie Mary - Married since August 1989

In 1992 John Gray wrote *Men are from Mars and Women are from Venus*. This has become a catch phrase used to describe the difficulty in understanding men and women.

There is an old story of a genie offering a man one wish. The man said "I'm afraid to fly, make me a bridge to Hawaii so I can drive there."

The genie responded, "That's a massive undertaking, trillions of tons of raw materials and supports spanning the depth of the ocean... is there something else I can do?"

The man thought for a moment, then his eyes widened. "I'd like to understand my wife."

JASON AND KELLI ANDERSON

The genie sighed deeply. "Would you like one lane or two?"

Driving my dad to lunch I spoke, "Fifty years of marriage this year, dad..." I stated matter of fact. He and my mom were crossing the half-century marker later that month. Then came the question. I paused for tension. "I remember growing up and seeing some good fights. Now I only see the joy. What is the secret to 50 years and happy?"

Without even pausing to think he furrowed his eye brows exactly as he does when he's teaching at the pulpit, "Two things." His right hand flashing the peace sign at the windshield. I could almost see the imaginary pulpit in front of him. "First, realize that understanding your wife is in fact possible, then pursue it. Second, I decided I wanted to give your mom the best life possible, and somehow, I ended up with exactly that. I have the best life I could have dreamed of."

Understanding your wife is possible. Pursue it. You might respond, "My wife is crazy. Unreasonable. Illogical." No she isn't. She is super smart. You aren't digging deep enough. If she is acting crazy it is because you missed something. Try again.

"I just don't get my husband. How could he possibly not (fill in the blank) ???" Your husband is a brilliant treasure. There is something going on here. Dig deeper.

Principle 16: Understanding your spouse is possible, pursue it.

Remember when you were dating, and you said to your friend, "Man, she gets me, you know what I mean. She totally understands me." Yeah, it felt that way didn't it. Being understood feels good. Later in marriage we say the opposite. "I just don't understand you." Ouch. It matters.

Over the next two chapters we will dive into the core foundational roles implanted in us by God for a man and a woman. I will jump start this concept in this chapter by revealing the fundamental roles of your spouse in the marriage as programmed by God in creation, then we will focus in on the man. In the following chapter we will focus on the roles of the wife. These roles can be clearly seen by God's design. This fundamental part of the design of a man and woman resides in the instinctive part of your spouse, programmed in creation by God. Your spouse is unique, no question, but there are roles of a man and a woman that are universal. If we know the role better, we can understand the programming. If we understand the programming, suddenly we can diagnose any problems.

For you and your marriage you can look at these roles and say, "Oh no, that just isn't us." Well maybe you're right, but for the sake of argument, consider the positions and where each may fit. These are working gears in a relationship. A team is most functional when the duties are separate but work together to make things more effective. We are used to things like "I'll cook dinner, but can you do the dishes?" Positions. Assignments. We each do something different that moves us toward the win. In my house I get the cars washed on Friday. That is one of my roles. I do trash. There isn't any confusion here. If the cans didn't make to the curb, we aren't wondering if we both forgot. It was I who forgot. Roles.

Understanding how something is supposed to work helps us diagnose the problem when it stops working. If we know how marriage is designed to work, then if it's broken down, we can check the symptoms and diagnose the problem. This way we can work on the solution. For example, If you don't know how a car works, and suddenly your car starts sputtering, it hiccups a few times, then the engine stops, you would have to guess what was wrong. Tow it. But a mechanic would ask, "Is there gas?"

You would say, "Yes. I think it is the battery. It has gas."

The mechanic would know that the symptoms are probably not battery related. He might respond, "Fuel pump!"

When the marriage is acting funny you look at the symptoms and make a diagnosis. So let's see how the man and woman are designed by God to function. Let's take a look at how the engine of each works.

I have categorized three roles for each.
Three fundamental roles of a man (masculine)

1. Provide
2. Protect
3. Lay Down Life (sacrificial love)

Three fundamental roles of a woman

1. Birth/Nurture
2. Influence
3. Believe in

A quick summary of this: A man provides food and shelter for the family. He protects the family, keeping them safe. He is willing to die for his family. A woman will birth and nurture what is planted in her. While a man leads by title, she will lead by influence. A wife is built to need to believe in her man. She is like the cheerleader on the field for the star quarterback. Sometimes she is like the coach that sends him in the game to win.

Remember the fairy tale romance? The fairy tales that survive through every generation touch these core fundamental values in us. They hit us right in the hopper, if you know what I mean. The knight rescues the damsel in distress. He is the prince. He has money, a house, and great horses. (Provider). He is strong and has a sword. (Protector) He risked his life for his love. (Sacrificial love). He is the instigator of the relationship. She is the reciprocator. He is the seed sower and she is the land. Why does he do it when he hasn't even really met her yet? He does it because she is beautiful, radiant. His heart is captured from the first moment he saw her. (Influence) She will love him because he loved her first, and gave himself up for her. She is birthing what he plants, and nurturing what she births, that is, his love. But it will take time. When another dragon appears, she calls for him, because, though she hardly knows him, she already believes in him. In some of our favorite love stories she doesn't just love him right away. It takes time for her to grow that love. In the case of Han Solo and Princess Leia, it was two movies later. She was rescued, sure, but she isn't weak or some push over. She has ideas and dreams and isn't fully convinced he is the right guy just yet. She has to birth that seed and it may take time. The prince quickly finds that she has the influence over him. Because he is so smitten with her, she is leading by influence. She is naturally influential. Do you see it? We watch it and we love it! So now let me go through each one carefully, and then we will look at how they interact.

Provider: Understand that your man was built by God to provide. Men hunt. We are the farmers. God said to Adam,

"You will toil the field," and He said to Eve, "You will birth.." A man makes sure the family eats. A wife can do this too, of course, but the man bears the ability, and therefore the responsibility. He hunts. It is why men are given the gift of focus. A man can block out all noise as we aim to hit the deer (or prepare for our presentation at work). A woman multi-tasks. She can think and feel at the same time. She can juggle two conversations, a drive through, a text message, and still make the correct turn. A man will have to make a U-turn when he finally realizes he is going the wrong way. But this is a gift.

A woman shooting a deer will wonder how this might make the baby deer feel when daddy deer doesn't come home. Men do not think and feel at the same time. This is why we may seem insensitive. It is also why when we get angry we can no longer put together a coherent sentence. It's why the wife can win so many fights. She can think and talk while she feels.

But this ability to hunt is how your husband won you. He was focused and determined. Now that focus may annoy you, but it is a gift. It will help him provide a great life for you and the children if you can get on board with this role that God has built him for.

The reason the damsel is attracted to the prince isn't because he has money. She isn't so superficial as that. The woman sees freedom from the worry and anxiety caused by lack. She sees safety. Before anyone can move on to accomplish anything they want to feel safe. When we feel unsafe it hinders all movement and growth. A marriage is the same. A strong provider helps bring a sense of security.

When I was a young man I noticed the girls were attracted to the boys with nice cars and nice clothes. I realize now that it wasn't the car or the clothes that caused the attraction. It was the expression of safety. Our Jesus is the husband to the church. One of the first things He promises is that with Him our needs will all be met.

Men, part of making marriage work is for you to step deep into this role. This will highlight a new attraction from your wife to you. These natural roles are part of our animal instincts for attraction. Some very deep part of your wife will be compelled in your direction.

A provider is a seed sower. We can see this by God's design. I want to address this more later, when we discuss the woman being a birther and nurturer. For now let's move on to the next role.

The man is also charged with the responsibility to be the protector of the family. Jesus, the Husband of the church is our Refuge. He is our shepherd. He is our Shield about us. He is our Strength and our Shield. Here again we see that a woman is attracted to safety, freedom from the fear of harm. Men are naturally bigger and stronger, without any working out at all. I Peter 3 tells us to, "treat your wife as the weaker vessel." Note, it doesn't say she is the weaker vessel. If you are married you certainly know that one by now. She is not weak! Really, the Bible is saying, "Don't let chivalry die." Some translations say to, "honor your wife as the weaker vessel." It is about honor. She is the queen. Queens don't open doors. Deal with it. She may not want you to treat her that way, but hey, go with God here.

And so there is a bump in the night. You were both sound

asleep but something isn't right. Alert now, you say, "Did you hear that? What was that?" Danger. *There is a rustling in the kitchen.* And so the husband says to the wife, "Go check it out, I'll wait here." Yeah, probably not. We get it. The man is up to protect the home and family in a flash. This is natural. Again, a man does not think and feel at the same time. For this reason he will have no problem ending the life of a would be attacker, and being able to eat a bowl of cereal five minutes later as he explains what happened to the police. Our brains are wired to handle a greater level of stress and intensity without panicking. This might cause our wives to believe we have no compassion. It might seem like we are numb to the emotions. A man's emotions aren't as loud. It is part of being a good protector. Believe it or not, we lie awake at night planning how we will respond to the attack if it ever happens. Weird, right? Something in us plays out the scenario in rehearsal mode. It isn't fear or faith for an attack to happen, it is more like a natural preparation for the role we have been given. Hey, ladies, we got you.

When a man stays fit and healthy, he is prepared as a protector. Staying in shape is part of the role of a man. Be tough. Be tireless. I used to wonder why girls would say, "I want a boy who is sensitive.." but then they would chase the bad boy. I was sensitive. But the girls were always hanging around the kid who was trouble. What was that? Safety. Deep down, without realizing it, the girls were attracted to the boy they could tell was a fighter, someone who could defend their honor. That doesn't mean you have to become the bad boy, but there is no question that the attraction of your wife will increase when she sees you staying fit and letting out your bad boy man from time to time. Momma likes it when you become the riled up protector. She may say she doesn't, but she does.

When a man gets all bruised and tired, achy, well, it's a turn off. "I'm so tired from work." Yeah, maybe you are, but jeez, don't tell her. Be Hugh Jackman from the Wolverine. He is tireless.

"My boss was mean to me, it's just not fair..." In this case you are being a victim and giving your wife your burdens. Give those to Jesus not your wife. Honor her. The Wolverine can be beaten to a pulp, but he just keeps getting back up. My wife says, "Don't lift that! Your back, you might hurt your back, honey!"

"Honey? I ain't no *honey*. I'm the wolverine right now. Baby, I have three words for you. *Super. Human. Strength.*"

Can you imagine Jesus coming into the church and saying, "It's not fair, everyone crucified me, they are all mean to me. I just don't know what to do?" The church needs Jesus to be our strength in time of need!

"Baby, you worked all day, you must be tired. Maybe we should just stay home." There is concern in your wife's eyes.

Be careful now. You may want to stay home. In fact, we guys usually do. But this, my friend, is a test. Did you give your best at work and now your family just gets the leftover lump of completely spent husband and father? Or, did you give your all at work, but you are tireless, revved up, and ready to go? She will be really, really, attracted to one of these. You guess which one.

The third role of a man is to love his wife sacrificially.

> Ephesians 5:25 (NIV) [25]Husbands, love your wives, just as Christ loved the church and gave himself up for her.

JASON AND KELLI ANDERSON

It doesn't tell wives to do this for husbands. So husbands, how did Christ love the church? Answer: He laid down his life. He died for her.

I was talking to a man who was married for over forty years before his wife passed. He told me this bit of wisdom. "I spent the first half of my marriage doing what I wanted. I got her to do what I wanted. It was quite frankly a marriage all about me. My wife was so gracious; she just let me do it. But I wasn't happy. Then I decided to make life about her. I let go of all the things I wanted and decided I would want what she wanted. When I gave her all of me, and gave up my own selfish wants, she gave it all back, but in a larger measure. That is where the happiness of a man thrives."

Hmmm. Jesus "Who for the joy set before him endured the cross." A man is built to lay down his life for his wife. She is built to have him prove that he will do it. Now I will put this in plain English. Write this one on your heart. If your wife thinks that anything outside of Jesus even remotely appears to be competing with her, she is programmed to make you give it up. She is programmed to have you prove she is more important than that. God did this. He did this to make sure His princess was loved the way she deserves to be loved. If you love your morning sleep, well, get ready to be an early riser for your wife. If you love golf with your friends, well, get ready for some fights that make absolutely no sense to you. "Can you come home and have lunch with me after seven holes?" *What? It's eighteen holes! Seven? Who plays seven holes?* You've got some more dying to do bro. But take heart, man, she will give it all back and with multiplication if you are willing to put her first.

Ephesians 5:23 (NIV) [23]For the husband is the head of the wife as Christ is the head of the church, his body, of which he is the Savior.

A husband leads by title. His leadership only functions properly, though, when his decisions are to benefit her at his own expense. This is also when a man is feeling happy and fulfilled. This is how Christ is the head of the church. Note the ending phrase of the Scripture "of which He is the Savior." This gear in your marriage clock is entirely shaped by the fullness of this word. Jesus' whole intention was to give up Himself for our benefit. He left nothing on the table. He died to every personal want and desire for us to have and share in everything that is His. He showed us clearly this as he bled in the Garden of Gethsemane and said to the Lord, "Not my will, but yours be done." Jesus let go of what he wanted in order to do something bigger for us. A man with this attitude will have no problem leading by the title God has given. You have to be willing to make her and your family number one.

My dad always told me, "When you get married you give up half your life. When you have children you give up the other half." Great advice.

Now then, once you prove that you would give up anything for her, she will stop asking you to. She will give it all back in good measure. Sacrificial love. Are you willing to give it all up for her? Would you sacrifice everything for the one you love? This will be one of your first tests after you say, "I do." In most marriages a newlywed wife will identify the very thing he loves the most in life and she will invent a test to make sure he values her most of all. God programmed her this way. She isn't even doing it intentionally. It is instinct. "You love me? Prove it."

Men, husbands, listen, you at some point must prove to yourself and her that she really is number one. There will be more tests as you go along, but if you keep in mind, "Oh, she just wants to make sure that she is number one." Then it will all make sense.

Doing well in your role will keep the gears in marriage moving smoothly. If one role goes haywire, it can be like a chain reaction right into a train wreck. I know a great man who left his newlywed wife. These are amazing Christian people. But he left. I asked him, "What's up?" So he explained he wasn't working and she told him that until he started trying to get a job she wouldn't sleep with him. Well, *that wasn't biblical,* so he left. Do you see the moving parts here? He needs to be a provider. She needs to know that he will stay with her no matter what she asks him to give up. Things begin to malfunction everywhere when we neglect our roles. When he left her, he let insecurity in the door. If she doesn't sleep with him, well, he leaves. Now she doesn't feel safe. Provide, protect, and sacrificial love. If he can get back in his roles, things will start to work again. Obviously she wants to sleep with him. He thinks she is acting *crazy.* Well maybe, but what is the root? I'm not taking sides here, I'm showing you how when one gear is out of place the whole engine goes bonkers. I spent some time teaching this man who loves the Lord about the roles. I helped him diagnose the real issue. The Spirit inspired this man to get back up on the cross and prove to that woman that there is nothing he wouldn't give up for her. *Lay down your life for her.* And get a job.

When a man is completely captured by a woman and will clearly give it all up for her because she is in first place in his life by a great distance, this is attractive to her. Very attractive. It is a compelling magnetic force for a woman to know that she is loved so deeply. Tell her you can't even breathe without her. Convince her that "Girl, you're every woman in the world to me." (Air Supply, had to be done.)

When a man abuses his wife it is a complete betrayal of the roles. He is to lay down his life for her, and protect her. If another man were to threaten her, he would step in to defend her. But now he has become the very thing he is designed to defend against. It is a true ultimate betrayal.

Principle 17: Masculine and Feminine Attraction.

Opposites attract. We are different. In order to get here mentally we need to let go of the way the world thinks of masculine and feminine as being bad. The world wants to blur this. But true attraction comes from being in our roles. The most instinctive attraction is masculine and feminine. Every intimate lover relationship is rooted in a masculine and a feminine attraction. Do not try and make the other be more like you.

Sometimes a wife will try to make her husband into her. We all do it I guess. We want the person we are with to think and react like we do. And so the struggle is, the man wants to give up everything for her. Suddenly he is becoming feminine like her. He does it because he doesn't want to fight. He does it because he loves her so much. He is so influenced by her she has taken the helm of the ship and his life, and he is just enjoying the ride. The problem is, she isn't going to be attracted to this feminine man. She creates a husband that she doesn't want. Suddenly she runs off with a guy who rides motorcycles, has a beard, and spits. Why? Because she isn't attracted to her husband anymore. This same scenario is true when a husband tries to turn his wife into one of the boys.

As we go through the roles of the woman now, I want you to see that the roles largely interact with feminine and masculine characteristics. These character traits are natural attractors. Each should fully embrace their own feminine or masculine traits and not mess with the others. Listen, guys, she doesn't think like you. She is woman. And the more you let her be woman, the hotter she will become to you. Ladies, your man is not feminine. The more you encourage him to be "all boy," the more you will find a deep, deep, attraction and passion for him. I'm not trying to disengage with your unique self and tell you to be someone you aren't. Instead, remember that the opposites not only attract, but complement and create power. In terms of electricity, the circuit requires both positive and negative. The circuit of your marriage increases in its power because of the differences. In looking at the differences recognize that the differences are what make you so much stronger together. Love the differences! Find the differences and exploit them to your relationship benefit. God put you together. And the most fundamental difference between you is the feminine and the masculine. I know the world doesn't like this conversation, but it isn't like marriage in the world is working, so we can easily abandon their strategy and take on God's design.

We have more to say about these three roles of men and the differences in the next chapter. As we look at the wife's God given roles we will also look at how it all works together.

Chapter Nine

Understanding Her

"I knew Wade was the one for me because it was the first relationship that I had been in, that I could totally be myself. He loved me with all his heart and made me feel like a princess. Our marriage works because we have never tried to change each other and we agreed that when we had disagreements that we would never resort to calling each other ugly names."
Michelle Anderson - Married since October 5, 1994

Now as I dive in here, let me reiterate what I just said by saying that the world's view of men and women is very, very, distorted. What has become politically correct to say about each has caused all sorts of new gender-blurring issues. The truth is, feminine doesn't have to be masculine in order to be strong. We must come to realize that being a strong man or a strong woman is to be strong in your role, confident in who and how God created you. We blur things when we decide that men are somehow superior, so a woman must become more manly so that she can be equal. If anything, science has told us that women really are mentally wired better than men, and men really are on average more athletic. These differences makes neither weaker, just different, and stronger together. Being a man isn't better, just different. Being a woman isn't better, just different. Real strength is the courage and confidence in who we are. It's okay to be different. Our differences make us stronger.

At the same time, the world desires to feminize men. Women become more masculine, and men become more feminine. The more this happens, the less either is attracted to each other. What causes the attraction to gain traction is so simple: Masculine is attracted to feminine. Feminine is attracted to masculine. Let go of what the world has said and remember, we may be in the world, but we are not of the world. The world's view of masculine and feminine wants to invade your marriage, but don't let it. It is the same for every generation. There are generations that treated women as insignificant and weak. This is still true in many of the countries I travel to. The same is happening in America today, but to men. God sees both men and women as significant, chosen, appointed, valuable, redeemed, righteous, holy and capable. We can do all things through Christ. Our differences make us unique and necessary!

Now let's look at the three roles of a woman. As we go through them I will show you how the roles can interact.

Three fundamental roles of a woman (feminine)

1. Birth/Nurture
2. Influence
3. Believe in

A woman is the *wombed-man*. She births the seed that is planted in her, and she nurtures what she births. This means she is a reciprocator or reflector of her man. The Bible calls her the "glory of her husband", meaning, she reflects the very best part of him. Her life is literally speaking about what her husband is like.

Seed must be planted in season. Women are seasonal with affection, love, intimacy, emotions, words, and in many other ways. There is a timing to when a seed can be planted, how it is planted, and how long it will take until there is fruit. In terms of a baby, we see that there must be intimacy to plant the seed, there is a right timing in her cycle, and it will take 9 months to produce the fruit. So while a man is in charge of the seed, the woman is in charge of the timing. "Not right now, I have a headache."

When it comes to timing we see that the wife falls into controlling the calendar. "We will go to your parents' house until noon, and then off to my parents' house until 7pm." We see that wives are often more in tune with the family calendar, the daily pickups. The man says, "Will you marry me?" She not only says, "Yes," but also is quite in charge of the when, the where, and the how the wedding will take place.

In the same way a man is planting seed in her via words and actions. Both words and actions are seed. Not everything will grow, and we aren't always sure when it all shows up, but beware husbands, use caution. Your words and actions are planting seed. If you sow love, you will eventually grow up in her a harvest of love. If you sow grace, you grow grace. If you sow harsh words, you will grow up harshness in her, and it will come back to you good measure, pressed down, shaken together, and running over.

Before you were the husband in her life, the man in her life, quite possibly her father or a prior husband, was tending this garden. There may be plants you are dealing with that you didn't plant. Be patient. When she gives you all of her, that garden is now yours for the planting and tending. In time it will reflect you. If you value her, she will grow value. If you neglect her, she will grow neglect. If you make her birthday amazing, she will do even more for you.

I was working with a couple where the wife would say the most horribly hurtful things I had ever heard. The man was also harsh with her, but not at the same level. Here was the simple truth he needed to hear: *She doesn't actually mean what she is saying* (she grimaced at me), *but instead, she is trying to make you feel how she feels inside.* He had planted criticism in her, hurtful words, and it was coming back to him but with multiplication. She birthed it. Seed is something a man can say and then it falls to the ground and he has let it go. But she grows the seed. On the surface it seemed the solution was for her to stop saying such hurtful things, but that was not actually the source. The source was his criticism. He exclaimed, "I've never said things like *that* to her! She told me she hates me and wishes I were dead!" Look, the gift God has given her is to grow and multiply seed. You, sir, have planted the wrong seed. Plant the right seed for a while and things will slowly change.

Listen, husbands, she doesn't mean a lot of the piercing words she said in that fight. She is trying to hurt you the way she is hurting. You have to find the pain that is in her garden. You can let go of those words she said and recognize the cry for value!

Maybe you've never planted harsh words in her. Well, someone did. Maybe it is her father, a brother, the old husband. It really doesn't matter who did it. What matters is, she is your garden now; help tend that garden. Shake off the negative or harsh words and plant some words of value. Love her without condition. A man might say, "I'm just talking to her the way she talks to me!" Don't do that. Just start planting a new garden, one filled with lovingkindness. She will grow you an absolute Eden if you will love unconditionally, that is, without any exception or need for return.

Now let me say it: Never say "divorce." Never. Do not let that word in your marriage. It is a destructive seed that wants to unlock pictures of the wrong future. If you have said it, pray it off and out of your marriage. Dig up that seed. Uproot that plant. It's not going to happen. You are stuck together, combined, one, and you really are better together!

Part of the process of birthing is "incubating." When a woman is impregnated, she will incubate, meaning, the wife is designed to think about the same thing for long period of time. She will replay a conversation fifty times. She has the gifted ability to really look at the seed that is planted and be intimate with that seed, in the same way the earth grows a seed or a woman incubates a baby. She surrounds it in three dimensions. A man has moved on, but she is replaying that story over and over. Wives, some stories replayed will only bring harm to your marriage. Capture your thoughts! Don't incubate things that will not move your marriage in the right direction. The Bible teaches us to "Guard your heart with all diligence." Men also have a heart that grows and incubates, but because of our design it is easier for a man to let it go.

Sometimes a fight is long gone, but she is still remembering it with vivid detail; the pain is alive and in 4K HD. She can still hear your words echoing. You might say, "Are you still thinking about that?" Listen, boys, before you let something out of your mouth, know that she will *still be thinking about that* a long time from now. This is a gift. For this reason a man should plant love. He can also get her thinking about how to handle little Timmy, who is acting up in class. Whatever you get her thinking about, she will stay with it for long after you stopped thinking, and she can produce wisdom in that situation. You could get her thinking about business ideas. Where a man may give up thinking about the solution to a problem, or often jump to the solution too early, a woman will incubate that issue. She will weigh carefully every scenario. It is a gift from God! She can read the room far better than the man. She can innately feel what others are feeling by seeing the small mood changes in others, the facial expressions, tone of voice, and body language.

She looks at you until she is sure you are listening, "When you said that I could tell you really hurt your mom's feelings."

"What?" He has that classic exasperated expression. "I know my mom, she is fine."

"Nope." She has brought out her crooked smile. "You're wrong, I saw it on her face."

And the wife is right yet again. It's a gift. Compassion and empathy live in the place of meditating and replaying moments. It's a gift, but it can also bring her pain. Reliving the moment of a tragedy plays out in her mind in great detail, and over and over again. You are understanding her now, and you recognize that because she is the *wombed-man*, she births. Maybe she has been grieving for sometime. You have been thinking, "Jeez, get over it." But now you see, it isn't something that is just "gotten over." Tend that garden. Help her let go of that movie. Plant hope in her. Plant healing words.

She is not only birthing what you plant, but then she is nurturing it. She is built to keep things going and growing. She is the only one built perfectly to keep that newborn alive. God has given her this great gift for nurturing new life, to get it going and growing. The man just doesn't have the equipment. The woman breast feeds and keeps that baby gaining weight and healthy. If you want anything to get bigger, give it to your wife. They nurture things. A man is designed to give up his life for his wife. A woman is designed to give up her life for her children. She sacrifices her body, her bones, and risks her very life to grow and birth a child. For this reason know that whatever she births, her instinct is to keep it alive.

I know a wife who stuck by her husband's side even though he was all about himself. He did whatever he wanted to do, and when he wanted to do it. She seemed to take third or fourth place in his life. He was angry often. She loved him. One day all those seeds he had sown had grown up in her heart. Like a light switch, she suddenly wanted out. She wanted him to hurt. She was angry and wanted him to feel how she felt. Monday she was fine, Tuesday she wanted a divorce. Now this husband really did love his wife, although he had been planting wrong. He gave it his all to save the marriage. He jumped through every hoop. I want to tell you he won her back, but he didn't. Once she birthed resentment, anger, neglect, and once she birthed the idea of living without him and what that would look like, she nurtured those things. She weened divorce. She kept all of that going and growing. She divorced him. Grow the good things and you will find the best life you can possibly imagine.

God built her this way. You sow kindness, and, boy, will you reap it. If you sow your attention and affection, she will take what you sow, multiply it, and then nurture it into an amazing relationship. It may take some time. I explained this to a man. He tried it for a week, and found that it just didn't work. Brother, a week is not enough time for a fruit tree to grow and begin to produce fruit. She is a birther. If you give her your whole life, she will give it back, multiplied, and she will nurture it and keep it going and growing. Plan on a four year commitment of good seed sowing before the garden begins to look different.

As a protector and a provider, a man will sometimes note that money is tight, and so he will say to his wife, "(harsh) What the..??? $120.00 on what??? I hope you enjoy it because now we won't be able to make our house payment..." Problem is, you just made two fundamental mistakes. First, you sowed a seed of fear, and you are the protector who is designed to make her feel safe. Second, you are the provider. If money is tight try wording it different. "Let's tighten our belts a bit, baby, so we can put some money in savings. What can we do to drop the spending?" Do you see the moving parts here?

As a seed-sower, a man, can never sow seed of burden and stress. We give our heavy yoke to Jesus, and then we take our wife's heavy yoke and give that to Jesus too. See, as a man you are built to protect her from stress. You are the peace-maker and load-taker.

For example, husbands, let's say your mom is stressing you out. Now if you come home complaining about your mom, you will sow seed in your wife to resent your mom, plus now your wife is stressed. Then, after you vented to your wife, you forgot about the whole thing with your mom. You shook it off. There is a problem though. Your wife is growing that thing. She will grow your anxiety, your stress, your burdens, your hurts, long after you have let them go. If you are worried that your wife is stressed out, check the seed. Pray for her, curse that anxiety plant at the root, and say what Jesus says, "You will never produce fruit again." Now speak good of your mom. Tell your wife of the great peace you are having, the hopes that are coming and plant happy seed.

The second role of the woman is to influence. A man leads by title, but a woman leads by influence. The Bible clearly states that a married couple is to "submit one to another." Even in the Old Testament there are many instances of women taking the leadership role over man, and by God's design. The New Covenant places us both in submission to each other. The wife recognizes the husband's title and God-given responsibilities. The wife also knows that she is not some puppy on a leash. She's brilliant. That man may lead this family right into the fire if she isn't able to warn him.

The woman is influential by design. Ladies, you have our complete attention from the time we are about twelve. I remember watching Gilligan's Island as a kid. There were many episodes when someone on the island needed to be persuaded to do something. The solution was usually to send in Ginger. Ginger was the glamorous movie star. She could persuade that man. She had the professors full attention when she wanted it, and he was putty in her hands. "That's not what you want to do." She would almost whisper, her fingers in his hair, her lips pouting.

"I don't?" He would mutter, completely hypnotized by her every word.

Now before you get all offended with this, just know that this is not objectifying women. Our society has made the idea of talking about the beauty of women taboo. But to God it is not. It is part of his gift to you. He didn't make men curvy, just the ladies. In this book we are merely identifying a design truth. God designed women to be radiant. You are beautiful, ladies. Men are built a bit clunky. The Bible says that Adam named her "woman." I wonder if he said it a bit different though. I imagine when Eve first came walking up to Adam, completely nude, he was like, "Whoaa, man!" (Woman) And his next response would have been, "What can I do for you?"

We love the movies when the man sees the girl, I mean really sees her, for the first time. The scene goes in *slow-mo,* and some 80's love song starts playing. He has forgotten everything going on around him in that moment. He could be in the middle of some heated battle but suddenly nothing but her matters. He will do anything she wants. Influence.

> Ephesians 5:25-27 (NIV) [25] Husbands, love your wives, just as Christ loved the church and gave himself up for her [26] to make her holy, cleansing her by the washing with water through the word, [27] and to present her to himself as a radiant church, without stain or wrinkle or any other blemish, but holy and blameless.

The bride is radiant. This is by God's design. According to Proverbs 31 God placed wisdom on your tongue. In the Bible there is a story of David, who wasn't king yet, and was watching the fields of a wealthy man. David and his men made sure to keep this man's land safe from theft. David sent some of his men to collect payment for his protection (almost sounds like the mafia), but the wealthy land owner refused. David's anger flared! David decided to kill the land owner and everyone in that household. Boys. The wealthy land owner was married to a wise woman named Abigail. When she got word of what her husband had done she did the math and knew something bad was about to go down. Abigail rushed to David bringing food and gifts, and mostly, wise words. She prophesied over David, knowing by the Spirit of God he would be king one day. She calmed him down and kept him from doing this awful thing. Later her husband died (but not at the hand of David) and David would marry this wise woman. Did you see her influence? Women can cause wars or avert wars. They are naturally influential over the men. The Bible is full of women who influenced entire nations.

Esther's beauty captured the king's heart, and she was able to change his mind about killing all of the Israelites in the land. How did she do it? Well, she made him a great meal, sat him down, and "Gingered" that man. "Chiefy weefy doesn't want to kill off the Israelites now does he?"

The king, hypnotized and a full belly, half asleep, "Nooooo, I don't want to kill Israelites..." And what happened? The relationship just got stronger.

A wife will want to nurture everything in her life including her husband. That man in your life is like a little boy, and you are going to want to treat him as such. But listen, ladies, your husband had a mom, and he doesn't want you to be his mom. It is super unattractive; biggest turn off ever. He wants to be your man, not your little boy! You loved to play with babies when you were a little girl, but you also loved to play Barbies and get out your Ken doll. These simple things reveal your programming and design that come from God. Your husband is Ken. He doesn't want you to change his diapers or look at him like he can't dress himself. Every time you treat him like a little boy, your influence goes right out the window. He left his mother for you, because he no longer needed a mother, but he needed a wife. What is my point? Don't lead by command, lead by influence.

Look, you are Ginger to your husband. He is enthralled by your beauty. Captivated. You have his complete attention whenever you want it. This is by God's design. A girl walks by and the boys stop working. They can't concentrate, they just stare. Sometimes the wife tries to lead by title, and this just creates a fight. Why? Because the roles are reversed. Ladies, you have all the influence you want, learn to use influence to steer things. When you just fire out a command, it really won't have the same effect. You command your children, no question, but you influence your husband. In fact, he loves it when you use that influence. It is very, very, attractive to him. Even a mom who attacks her post pubescent son finds a great battle. Why? Because a woman attacking a man (even though he is only fourteen years old) is dysfunctional. She must use influence now. She orders a child, but influences a man. So other men in that teen's life have to become the discipliners, because she becomes the influencer. A man has the leadership title, but it is dysfunctional for him to attack or order a woman because he is the protector and the sacrificial lover of her. Do you see the brilliance of God's Word here? We don't order each other, but we submit to one another in love. He leads through love and seed sowing, and she leads through influence.

You have captured that man's heart. Now he may not always act like it, but you have his heart. You have the ability to influence that man. It is part of your role. He is like putty in your hands.

The third role of a woman is to "submit." Now I said earlier it was to "Believe in," and that was so you would keep reading and not shut me down. *Submit? What is this, 1955?* Well, let us read what God has declared:

Ephesians 5:22 (NIV) [22]Wives, submit yourselves to your own husbands as you do to the Lord.

A man leads by title, and he needs you to push that title on him. He is capable. Sometimes a man will not be leading because society has trained him that he is dumb, slow, lazy, selfish, and a terrible leader. Men have been told since they were little that they are losers, can't dress themselves, and are not as smart as girls. Boys have been told they aren't as obedient and that they are a problem. Or maybe that man had no role model. Or maybe he just loves you so much he really does want you to make all the decisions. Or maybe he has noticed you are happier when you are running the show. It could be a billion things, but there is greatness in that man, and if a wife refuses the role of leader, and forces him to step into it, he will be great at it. He is built for it. When a wife accepts her role that man will step into his.

Now on to the key phrase, "Submit...as you do to the Lord." You submit in the same way you submit to Jesus. How does Jesus require we approach him? All He asks is that you believe in Him. The key to eternal life is to believe in Jesus. You have never even met Jesus in the flesh, but you believe. You believe what He says. You believe He loves you. You believe Jesus saves you. Your husband isn't Jesus, but you are to submit to him in the same way you submit to Jesus. Why do you listen to Jesus? Because you believe in him. In others words, one of your roles is to submit to your husband because you really and truly do believe in him. Then, your influence and brilliance kick in because of the next truth; you were given to him because he needs your help. He needs it. Without you it is not good. That is what God said. "It is not good for man to be alone. I will make him a help-mate." He needs help. This is not a dictatorship. You submit one to another. It is a team. He leads by title, you lead by influence.

I imagine God looked down at Adam before he had made Eve and noticed him just sitting there.

"What is Adam doing now?" His face and hands questioning in annoyance as he peers from the throne.

An angel replies, "Well, he's been sitting there most of the day. He threw rocks in the pond for like an hour. Then a nap. Really, not a whole lot going on."

He needs help! So God sent him someone that likes to be busy and go hiking. Grrrrr.

"I don't think that's what he is going to want…" Gabriel states without emotion.

Michael chimes in, "Well, make her crazy smart, pretty and naked. Boom."

When a woman truly believes in her husband watch out. Did you know believing in your husband is a choice? You just choose to believe that he is your Wolverine. He is your Superman. He is the strongest, fastest, smartest, most anointed godly man on the face of the planet. Believe it, and help him pull all of that out of the clay pot that is sitting in the lazy boy chair snoring.

Now let us look at an interaction that can cause a mess in the marriage based on these roles. See if you can identify the problem quickly.

A woman is mad because her husband is off to work early and home late. He is trying to get ahead in the job, and giving his *all* five days a week. Sometimes six. She is feeling like work is more important than her. Her need to be number one in his life forces the test. She hates his job and there is a fight if he is home late. This is a super common scenario.

A man must be the provider. He is trying to be a great provider. So the wife has pitted two roles of the man against each other. On one hand he needs to prove that his wife is most important. On the other hand, he knows that diligence and faithfulness at work is part of being a provider. I mean, if he stays home, they lose the job, and then eventually they lose the home.

The point I want to make here is that neither husband nor wife can give up on a role, even for the sake of another role. All three roles for each are necessary. A woman cannot be asked to give up her desire to have a baby because the man says there isn't enough money.

A jealous man will try and control how his wife looks. His concern is that she is leaving the house "too pretty." One of her roles is to be influential – radiant. Pray the Lord remove jealousy from the relationship. Jesus has overcome!

These basic roles of both the husband and wife are instinctive in each, and are simple and easy to understand. Meditate on these roles. In my first few years of marriage it was these roles that helped both of us sort out where we each fit best in our relationship. Even if you are alone in your search for a better marriage, that is, your spouse has no interest in reading this, take hope! If one spouse anchors to their roles, the other will by nature make the adjustment. If one refuses to be dysfunctional, things will become functional, albeit with a bit of painful maneuvering. Grease those gears up with love and grace and you'll be just fine. And look, understanding is, in fact, possible!

Chapter Ten

Seasons in Your Marriage

"We had a relationship with the kids, but also a relationship outside of the kids. We would go on dates and trips just the two of us."
Mary June Collins – Married since August 19, 1971

Every season of marriage is going to be different, in the same way winter is different than spring. A tree responds differently to the changing temperatures and atmosphere. Your marriage will be the same. When you are first married but have no kids yet, well, marriage is quite different than for the couple who has four children under the age of five. Quite different. Different rhythm. Different communication. Different energy levels.

Now what makes us different from a tree is that we are capable of planning ahead. A farmer plans for the next season. If it is suddenly planting time and he hasn't even tilled or fertilized, he is going to be stressed out getting things ready. In the same way, be aware of the next season so that you don't have to freak out on each other in the marriage trying to hold things together.

The principles throughout this book will help you have smooth transitions and success in each season. But I still want to talk about them in hopes it will have us all thinking about how we can be successful in the next season.

In this chapter I will talk about three seasons of marriage. The first is marriage before you have kids. The second is marriage with kids. The third is like the first, there are no kids. They all moved out.

In a traditional marriage there are no kids at first. So for some of you, well, you were married and already had kids, or she brought kids into the marriage, or he did, or whatever. But for some, you were married and there weren't any kids. The first year of marriage is laying the foundation.

> Deuteronomy 24:5 (NASB) [5]When a man takes a new wife, he shall not go out with the army nor be charged with any duty; he shall be free at home one year and shall give happiness to his wife whom he has taken.

Well that is a crazy concept. Today many do not even take a honeymoon, let alone a year off. I mean, life moves fast and we are all very busy. Still, this should make you pause. When laying the foundation of your marriage take caution. This foundation will be what gets you through the storms and the hard times. When there is a love famine in year number three, those strong roots you developed in the first year will find nourishment deep in the earth and you will be able to maintain. So what can you do to get that first year right?

I don't know, but I think you can see it requires a slowdown.

In my first year of marriage, Hank Meyer, a seven-foot-tall brilliant teddy bear of a man sat me and my wife down for a talk. He crossed one massive leg over another, his brown disheveled hair semi parted on the side with his bangs tangling into his thick glasses. He smiled as he began.

"Now Jason, in the Bible days a man would take a year off to just be married. He gave all of his attention to his wife. Now, you are teaching the children's 6th grade Bible study, you sing for the children's worship, you drum for the worship team, you have a band that practices three nights per week..." He paused. He stared at me. Then he slowly pursed his lips and stretched his massive arms, palms up, as if to say *what are you doing?* Then there was silence.

What Hank was so brilliantly telling me was to slow down, back out of some stuff, and just be married for one year. So this is what I did. We both did. We would no longer be gone every night of the week. We took weekend trips just the two of us. We watched TV at night. We were just about each other. We became really comfortable, just the two of us. This is preparing you for children. Now if you didn't get to experience this time, just know that there is a goal you need to get to. The goal is to be all about each other when time permits. Don't be so busy until that foundation is established. If you haven't taken the time yet to do this, and maybe you are in year thirteen, well, it isn't too late. Why not take a year to slow down and really establish things?

In this first season you are figuring out how your extended

family is going to work into your marriage. Moms and Dads are doing their best to micromanage your relationship but you are "leaving your father and mother." Here you are setting some of the traditions of where you will be and with whom on holidays.

Season number two: Children

Principle 18: Who was here first?

Once children are added to the marriage everything changes and will remain changed forever. In a traditional family after a few years of laying the foundation of the relationship the baby arrives. Here a woman has given up her life for the new life. Husbands have found intimacy has become more sporadic. Wife is a mommy now, and switching the mom hat and the lover hat isn't all that easy. Sleep becomes a precious commodity. You went to your favorite restaurant but the baby was not having it. There was plenty of crying.

How we discipline or raise children suddenly becomes a new fight. How the in-laws play into all of this creates all kinds of tension. As children grow things get busier. There are soccer practices way too many nights, and for some reason the league placed you not with the team that practices at the park across the street, but instead, twenty minutes away. *Did you pick up the violin?* This is when a man finds out that sometimes what his wife wants isn't always said so clearly.

It's ten thirty at night and the kids are finally asleep. The husband just climbs into bed with a groan, pulls the covers up when suddenly the wife comes stomping in, "We are out of milk." Now she is just staring. This isn't technically a question or request which would require a reply. However, if you use a translator, say a man who has been married for many years, what she said was, "Go to the store and get some milk." Yeah, this fight doesn't happen until after you have kids.

Now, this is not a parenting book, but if you want to win in this season, you should get one. Maybe pick up a few. Many marriages end because the dynamic with kids is just enough additional strain for someone to want out. The goal throughout all of this is simple. Peace. Your house must be a place of retreat. Your home is anointed by God to be a resting place. Peace is often the result of knowing the right answers. This means great information. I recommend *Baby Wise* for newborns, *Train up a Parent* for children, and for teens – *Yep, I Have Teens*.

Having a successful marriage once the kids start coming requires us to answer this question correctly: Who was here first? The two of you were here first, then the children came. The children are born into an existing family, that is, two married people. So the kids have to learn to fit in to what they were born into. This will raise healthy flexible children and keep the marriage solid. We sometimes want to put those kids into first place but this will create two problems. First, the kids begin to believe the world revolves around them. This is a child-centered home. This is a key ingredient to raising unhappy selfish children. Second, there is nothing more important to the kids than mom and dad loving each other. Nothing. So if you don't keep the marriage in first position everyone loses. Now having said that, I spoke to a man who told me that he was worried about his wife. She was putting the children before him. It was like the children were more important. He was all about her and she was all about the kids.

Surprise, this is actually right. She is designed to give up everything for the kids. He is built to give up everything for his wife. She is not told to do this for her husband. If a man rejects or abuses his children, the wife will divorce him to protect the children. She is built to do that. The children really do come first in her life. (Until the kids are married, then you gotta let 'em go, mamma.) For the husband to gain his wife's undivided attention he will have to help her with the kids, settle things so that she is able to relax and take off the mom hat more often. When the kid duties are handled, pantry is stocked, and decisions about where you will spend thanksgiving has been made, she can return to her wife role.

What if you got married but you each both had kids from a prior marriage, or one of you did, now what? The principle actually still applies. The math here gets complicated. The marriage must eventually be first, but because there are existing kids, and they came first, there will need to be a slow process to move marriage into that position. Move too fast and the kids will feel quite violated. Why? Because it goes against the natural order of things. The order in this case is, the kids came first. *So who is the new guy?* Be patient with each other here. When a man demands to be in first place, she may just bail. That is not a sacrifice she is built to make. A man however may quickly move his new wife into first position, but again, at the expense of the children who are going to feel abandoned. Pray. God has the right timing for you.

Season #3 - All moved out we had a life without the kids

This third season is called "empty nest." The egg appeared, then it cracked, hatched, and a little bird flew away. Now what?

When the kids start moving out there is a natural order that God has designed. Here the second born is able to experience what it is like to have some extra attention and be the oldest. If you have four kids, as each graduates to life on their own, the remaining kids get more of mom's and dad's time; time that they couldn't get when they were younger. When only two kids had been born, those two received all your time. When number three came, well, *hey, where is that third kid?* And so our psychologists talk about the forgotten child, or the middle child. But the natural order of things eventually has your youngest child being the only child, since the rest moved out. This is how God designed it. Each child gets that focus and attention. Embrace this! Plan for this. Then, one day, when the last one is thirty-five years old (I'm kidding), they are all gone.

Empty nest can create a mess in marriage. The key to avoiding this is to have a relationship with each other that is outside of the children. Have time where it is just the two of you. If all of your time is with the kids then when they are gone, your marriage will lose it's identity.

When the last kid moves out that commodity called "Time" that has been missing for the last twenty five years or more is back, and it is back like a flood. You will have time. When you were young and didn't have kids you seemed plenty busy. But now, after seeing how busy life really can be with kids, you are going to be hit with time, and it will be in abundance. Even as both husband and wife may maintain full time work, you won't know what to do with your time. What's my point? Have a plan. Start that plan before the last one moves out. Now is the time to start that business idea. You have the wisdom and years of experience to really do something. Many people retire or wish they could, but I'm saying to do the opposite. Start planning what you will do when the last one moves out before they move out.

> Proverbs 29:18 King James Version (KJV)[18] Where there is no vision, the people perish:

Have a vision for your future. Remember in our earlier chapters where we were digging around to find each other's desires? Do this. Do this and then make a plan. Have a vision to keep going. Going into your next season you should be excited and hopeful. When our marriage has a vision, it is full of life and direction. But when the last kid moves out, it is a heart-breaking event. If there is no hope on the horizon, the marriage is going to run into a tough spot. God has a long life planned for you. He promised 120 years. Remember all the things you couldn't do because there was no time? Remember those things? Well, now you have the time.

I know a married couple who were perfect when the kids were around, but could not figure out who they were when the kids moved out. Things fell apart fast. The wife was down, she began to live in the past often finding regrets for not having spent more time with the kids. He buried himself in his work, because he couldn't take the complaining. They lived out the rest of their lives married, but they were miserable. This story happens often. Many times the story ends in divorce. The wife is ready to move into the next realm of desires and dreams, dreams that were on the back burner for too long, but the husband wasn't ready. The two had grown apart. Boom, she's gone.

Having a plan before the kids move out will help tremendously. Spend time with friends, family, and grandchildren, and mostly, with each other. Pursue desires and dreams.

Empty nest is also around the time when our hormones and health get funky. Your physical body may have been through the ringer raising all these kids and paying for their education. Whatever your health situation, be aware that your hormonal imbalance can greatly impact your moods, your desire for intimacy, and your energy levels. This is not a medical book, but for the sake of your marriage, get proactive with having some blood work done. Ask your doctor for tests to find out what hormone deficiencies you may be having, and what other things need to be paid attention to for your health.

I know a man who after the last kid moved out lost his sexual drive entirely. This was making a mess of the marriage as the wife was feeling rejected and unattractive. In a blood test he found that his testosterone levels were freakishly low. The doctor prescribed something to help, and within days, things were already better. He started working out again, had energy, and that passion and spark returned to his marriage.

God has an amazing plan for your life, a plan for hope and a future. He has a plan for your marriage. I believe that you have made a giant leap towards all that he has for you, a leap into a marriage that flows with milk and honey, a friend who will stand with you to the end and a lover who is passionate for you, who burns with hunger for your attention.

Chapter Eleven
Final Remarks

"I had to fight off many suitors including my brother for Angie. We knew we loved GOD and each other deeply. We decided that that love would prevent anything from coming between us and separate us."

PJ and Angie Priore – Married since May 15, 1965

In this book we have learned primarily to speak a different language in our marriage. How the world speaks is different than how we speak. Our marriage deserves a new language so that we can have a different experience.

We learned first that we speak a *language of desire* to each other. This is when we are intentional about sharing our wants with each other. Here we dream and talk about our future together. In discovering each other's desires we become far more equipped to reach toward fulfillment. In this we also learned the language of listening. Listening empowers understanding, and is a completely lost language in today's fast paced society.

We talked about the *language of remembering*. Where the world remembers the wrongs, we remember the rights. We are learning to remember what God remembers. God does this for His own sake so that our relationship with Him can be close and strong. In the same way, what we remember can build up walls, or tear down walls. We can find ourselves closer to our spouse, or we can push our spouse further away, all by what we choose to remember.

We put kindness into our communication. The *language of kindness* is far from the harsh language we are surrounded with. Kindness is a magnet in our love, in that it draws us closer together. If you are harsh with each other, it places a wedge in the relationship. Choose kindness.

We also learned the secret *language that can elevate your spouse*. Our words can tear down, or they can build up. If we want elevation in our marriage, then we learn to elevate each other. Here we encourage, lift up, complement, and speak of the future with hope. While the rest of the world is tearing each other down with their words, we have learned a new language, one that lifts others up.

Moving your marriage into God's house immerses you in the language of the Kingdom of God. God talks different than us, and He is getting different results. When we learning the *language of God* and His patterns for home and family invade our home, bringing the things of God into our realities.

We also learned the forgotten *language of affection*. Here we speak thousands of words without even saying a word. It is the communication of a gentle touch, a soft kiss, or an evening spent under a blanket all wrapped up in each other enjoying a movie. Part of this language of affection plays heavily into learning and speaking the *language of passion*. We are declaring from the mountain tops the beauty of our lover. We use words to express our feelings to each other. We dress to impress the other, valuing their gaze and attraction.

We also learned the *language of us*. This is no longer the language of our history, our culture, or our past. It is no longer the language of me, or my, or mine. It is the language we learn together, words that the two truly understand and share. It is the language of us, we, and ours.

We learned to speak a new *language of our marriage expectations*. We aren't in prison, but we are free. We learned to say *my marriage isn't just surviving, my marriage is thriving.*

"We wish you the very best journey in this life. We pray your marriage is fulfilling, far beyond your wildest expectations. We pray that you would be Happy and Married."
Jason and Kelli Anderson – Married since June 12, 1993

Where will you spend eternity?

If you're reading this and you've never given your life to God, you can do it right now. In John chapter three is a story of a man who visited Jesus in the night and asked how a person can get eternal life. Jesus' response is that *God so loved the world that He gave His one and only son that **whoever** **believes** in Him would not die but would have everlasting life*. You see, it is about a choice to **believe**. It is not about what you do. If you want to give your life to the Lord right now, just say this simple prayer and mean it. Mean it in your heart and you can be saved.

Dear Father God, I ask you to forgive me of all my sins, and ask you, Jesus, come into my life, come in to my heart, be my Lord and my Savior, and baptize me in the Holy Spirit, in Jesus' name, Amen.

If you said that for the first time, find a church. You were born again into the family of God; now go join that family, gather with the believers. The very key to the timing and speed of your growth will hinge entirely on you hearing the Word of God in God's house. This is God's pattern. Six days a week you are out working, doing your thing, and one day a week you are in God's House. Six days you hear from the world who you aren't, what you can't have, and what you can't do. It's important that one day we hear who our Creator says we are, what He says we can do, and what He says we can have. We get our heads put back on straight, get some hope stirred up; we are reminded to love and to forgive. Be in church. Do not let satan deceive you into thinking it just isn't important. It is. Church is the very Bride of Christ.

And I want you in the church where I preach. I do.

Made in the USA
Columbia, SC
21 February 2020